THE PRACTICAL POCKET GUIDE TO
ACCOUNT PLANNING

CHRIS KOCEK

YELLOW BIRD PRESS

The Practical Pocket Guide to Account Planning is a work of nonfiction. Nonetheless, some names and personal characteristics of individuals or events have been changed in order to disguise identities. Any resulting resemblance to persons living or dead is entirely coincidental and unintentional. Endorsements and advice from industry professionals are the opinions of the cited commentators and do not necessarily reflect the opinions of their agencies.

Copyright © 2013 by Chris Kocek

Published in the United States of America by Yellow Bird Press

ISBN: 978-0-9892849-0-5

Library of Congress Control Number: 2013937810

Awesome World of Advertising illustrations by Jean-Francois Dumais
All other illustrations by Lin Zagorski

www.practicalplanningbook.com

Cover design by Rebecca Pollock

Book design by Lin Zagorski

10 9 8 7 6 5 4 3 2 1

Praise for **THE PRACTICAL POCKET GUIDE TO ACCOUNT PLANNING**

"This book is perfect for anyone who wants to answer the following question: What does an account planner do and should I become one? *The Practical Pocket Guide to Account Planning* is an outstanding review of the sorts of questions planners ask every day and what it takes to be able to answer them."

— **Eddy Hodgson, Brand Planning Director, The Richards Group**

"This guide dissects every piece of the "planner puzzle" to help new and aspiring planners get off on the right foot. With simple, straightforward prose, it's an easy to understand, honest assessment of an often complex profession. I wish I had this book to help me navigate the world of planning over a decade ago."

— **Esty Gorman, Director of Strategy, Iris Worldwide New York**

"Finally, a no bullshit take on a discipline that — decades in — still lacks proper definition. *The Practical Pocket Guide to Account Planning* is the ideal primer for anyone considering a career in Account Planning."

— **John Gibson, VP/Planning Director, The Martin Agency**

"A whirlwind tour through the real-world landscape of agency planning. *The Practical Pocket Guide to Account Planning* is essential for the next generation of strategists."

— **Jim Firestone, Chief Strategy Officer, T3 Austin**

"This is the perfect companion to *Truth, Lies and Advertising: The Art of Account Planning*. When I received an advance copy, I immediately shared it with a few lucky students and mentees. *The Practical Pocket Guide to Account Planning* is full of useful examples, practical tips and tangible scenarios that tackle the mysteries surrounding the ever-changing 'planning' discipline."

— **Clay Langdon, Strategic Director, McGarrah Jessee Austin**

"Planning is the one last agency function without detailed guidelines. *The Practical Pocket Guide to Account Planing* gives all the details you need without the typical overcomplication."

— Torsten Gross, SVP/Group Planning Director, Deutsch New York

"It's more than a guide. It's a great door for anyone who wants to sneak their head in and discover the basics of Account Planing in a very complete way."

— Carlos Arcos, Executive Director of Strategic Planning, La Comunidad

"Every mission must begin with the basics—all the parts and pieces on the table. *The Practical Pocket Guide to Account Planning* does exactly that, giving students a practical start. Ultimately, it's up to each Planner on their own to live an interesting life and bring their unique ideas and experiences to bear for their Clients. So put this guide in your back pocket and then go make some magic."

— Matt Goldberg, SVP/Group Planning Director, BBDO New York

"A wonderful little gem. *The Practical Pocket Guide to Account Planning* is the perfect tool kit to get young planners off and running."

— Ole Pedersen, Chief Strategy Officer, Strawberry Frog New York

"A true to life picture of the mysterious world that is advertising. I wish I'd had such a guide book when I started in the industry. I would have spent more time doing productive things and less time trying to work out what the heck was going on."

— Chris Potts, SVP/Group Planning Director, BBDO New York

"Delivers a genuine telling from an active practitioner's POV. It's a unique take on the craft of Account Planning in the U.S. today."

— Brent Vartan, Partner, Chief Strategy Officer, Deutsch New York

Endorsements from industry professionals are the opinions of the cited commentators and do not necessarily reflect the opinions of their agencies.

To my mom,
who always taught me
to be anything but practical

CONTENTS

PART IV: TRICKS OF THE TRADE

WHAT KIND OF TOOL ARE YOU?

Several years ago, I was working for a big agency
on a major home improvement retail brand and
one night, while we were out having dinner with
our Clients, we ended up playing a game called,
"What kind of tool are you?"

The Account Director, it was determined, was a
hedge trimmer. The Account Supervisor was a
weedwacker. The Clients described one of their
own as a sledgehammer. But when it came time
to describe me, the Account Planner, no one was
quite sure what to compare me to. Eventually,

after much debate, it was decided by group consensus that I was the equivalent of some mysterious and somewhat complicated 19th century tool that looked impressive, but that left you wondering what exactly its purpose was and how to use it.

This wasn't the first time I'd heard of people's confusion regarding the role of Account Planning. From Clients to Account Directors to Creatives to Planners themselves, there's a great deal of mystery surrounding the profession. Perhaps it's because even the people who work in Account Planning have no single, standardized definition. If you ask ten different Planners about the role and responsibilities of Account Planning, chances are you'll get ten different answers. The truth is most Planners have zig-zagged their way across a number of professions – journalism, design, theatre, comedy, film – and one way or another, they just ended up in the business.

So what is it exactly that Planners do? How do we find those hidden insights lurking in the corners of human psychology and human behavior and turn them into something actionable? That's what this book is all about. Because at the end of the day, Planning isn't that mysterious. It's a very specific set of skills, with compassion and curiosity at its core. At its most basic, Planning is the craft of storytelling. And as all great storytellers know, with enough practice and enough refinement, it's a craft that can be raised to the level of an art.

That said, this book isn't about the art or theory of Account Planning. It isn't about how Account Planning should work in an idealized world. It's a practical guide that gives you a behind-the-scenes perspective of what Planning is all about, with plenty of real-world examples, so that you can see how ads, campaigns, and brands get built on a day-to-day basis.

PART 1: ORIENTATION

WHAT'S IN A NAME?

JOB DESCRIPTIONS VS. REALITY

WHO'S WHO AT THE AGENCY

WHAT'S IN A NAME?

There are more than 8,000 agencies in the world today, which means there are a lot of Planners out there. Account Planners. Brand Planners. Strategic Planners. Behavioral Planners. Marketplace Planners. Don't be intimidated by all the names. In many cases, it's just nomenclature. Different agencies come up with different names for their Planners because they can use those clever names to differentiate themselves from other agencies in the marketplace. The truth is they're all pretty much doing the same thing.

However, there are genuine differences between the following kinds of Planners:

→ **Account Planners** are typically thought of as "the voice of the consumer." Our job is to put consumers at the center of the communications process and figure out what exactly the brand needs to say so that consumers and influencers will actually pay attention to our message and ultimately change their behavior.

→ **Media Planners** are responsible for figuring out the best possible touchpoints so that the campaign will reach consumers at the most influential moments. If Account Planners are responsible for figuring out what we need to say, then Media Planners are responsible for figuring out where and when we need to say it. That said, media planning and creative development go hand in hand and are constantly influencing each other. Sometimes a media plan can influence a particular creative idea. In other cases, a creative idea can lead to an entirely different and completely unique media plan.

→ **User Experience Planners** (or UX Planners for short) are a new breed of Planner who typically get their start in the world of Information Architecture (website wireframes, app design, user-flow, etc.). As more channels become interactive, campaigns are less about messaging and more about dialogue. That's where UX Planners come in. To create these continuous feedback loops across channels, UX Planners must have an intimate understanding of consumer decision processes and the technology consumers are using.

These days, a number of people in the industry believe that traditional Account Planners and UX Planners will cross-pollinate at some point and become some kind of Super-Planner, a delicious hybrid, like a Tangelo or a Plumcot. Who knows? Either way, no matter what adjective comes at the front of your Planning title, the most important thing you can do is be collaborative and work closely with everyone around you – creatives, developers, information architects, account directors, interns - to get a better understanding of the attitudes, perceptions and behaviors of the consumers your brand is trying to talk to.

Now, if you want to know about the history of Account Planning, or why Account Planning was created in the first place, there's a great entry waiting for you on Wikipedia. But if you want to know what it is Account Planners actually do on a daily basis, then keep reading.

JOB DESCRIPTIONS VS. REALITY

Every day in Planning is a little different. The only routine you really have is keeping your fingers on the pulse of culture. That means reading, observing, experiencing, and writing. All the time. Even on weekends. That's why you always see Planners carrying around a pocket-sized notebook wherever they go. Because you never know when an interesting observation or an insight might strike. That said, if you want to get a broad sense of what Planners are expected to do, here's a compilation of actual Planning job descriptions from different agencies.

Our Strategists merge research, best practices, latent trends and intuition to craft high-level plans and accompanying tactics that aid in the creation and communication of brands. A great Strategist is first and foremost a generalist, someone who can cite Plato as well as discuss the latest reports on economic activity. We expect our Strategists to be voracious media consumers, especially new media.

CORE DUTIES/RESPONSIBILITIES

Own 1 or 2 key accounts, on which you will:

- *Develop single-minded creative briefs that inspire Creative and UX teams*

- *Be a part of daily strategic discussions – often as the lead voice in the room*

- *Own various qualitative and insight-based deliverables to drive customer understanding*

- *Act as liaison between Media Planning and Creative*

- *Play an active role in Client presentations and overall strategic guidance through the life of a campaign*

- *Produce intellectual property in the form of White Papers, Reports, Blog Entries and Social Media Content*

REQUIRED SKILLS/KNOWLEDGE/EXPERIENCE

- *Curious and resourceful; comfortable designing and implementing qualitative research, conducting consumer and stakeholder interviews, and uncovering unique sources of insight*

- *Demonstrated ability to connect strategy to execution*

- *Capacity to package information in clear, concise and impactful ways*

- *Knowledge of the digital marketing and advertising landscape, and their impact on Account Planning*

- *Strong interpersonal skills, a positive attitude, and the ability to thrive in a collaborative agency environment with multidisciplinary teams*

- *Superior oral, written and interpersonal communications skills and presentation skills*

- *The ability to successfully manage multiple internal and external initiatives/projects in a deadline driven environment*

- *Global sensibility – you know where Antwerp and Mumbai are*

- *A strong serving of humility, humanity and doubt*

Now you know what a Planner actually does, right? OK. Maybe not. To give you a more specific idea of how those job descriptions translate into actual Planning output, here are some real assignments I've been asked to do during my Planning career:

→ Explore how the definition of "helpful" has changed over the past thirty years and identify new ways for the Client to personalize their particular brand of helpful in the digital age.

→ Research brand jingles that have undergone successful modernization and provide Client with recommendation on whether or not to keep, modernize, or kill Client's historic brand jingle.

→ Write White Paper on buy local/made in the USA trend and provide agency POV/recommendation on whether or not this trend could be used to the Client's advantage.

→ Develop concept statements/messaging territories for upcoming brand campaign to be tested in focus groups.

→ Identify and rank A-list celebrities for upcoming brand ambassador/celebrity spokesperson position.

→ Develop brand pyramid so that internal Clients can see "at-a-glance" how different campaigns, partnerships, and celebrity spokespeople ladder up to the current brand positioning.

→ Develop sustainability platform for a retail brand that includes platform name, communications hierarchy, merchandising opportunities, and product innovations.

→ Develop creative brief and potential themes for rebranding conference rooms at Client headquarters.

→ Provide agency recommendation on how best to structure, staff and implement a social media strategy that includes social media monitoring capabilities.

→ Field an online user experience survey to understand why people go to key areas of a brand's website and what they learn about the brand when there.

→ Work with the Client to develop a strategic process (from assignment definition to research decisions to insights to positioning) to improve the quality of Client briefs and insight work.

After looking at this list of assignments, you can probably understand why a lot of people are confused as to what exactly Planners do. We're asked to do so many things that it's fair to say we do it all. We're flexible. We're versatile. We're like Swiss Army Knives. To be a good Planner, you've got to be ready for just about anything.

WHO'S WHO AT THE AGENCY

If you get hired by a big agency, chances are, you won't get a very good agency orientation. Or, it'll be so fast that you won't actually remember any of it. You'll shake a lot of hands, you'll review a few packets of information, and then you'll be shown to your office, which will be sparsely furnished with a desk, a filing cabinet, a computer and a phone. You might have a roommate or you might have the office all to yourself. And, if your experience is anything like mine, after the first couple of hours, it'll be time to dive in to the details of your Clients' business.

So before you put your nose to the grindstone on that first day, here's a bird's eye view of what a large ad agency looks like and where you, as a Planner, fit inside it:

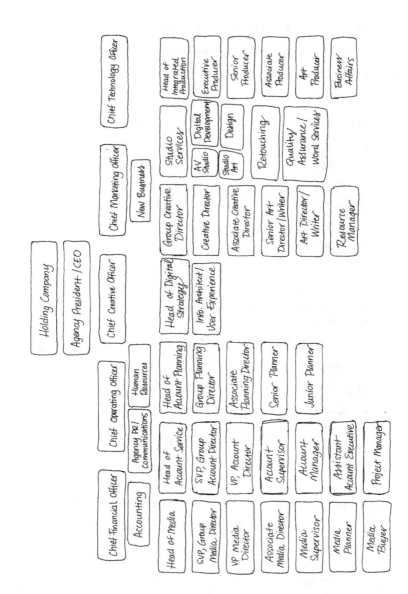

Of course, this org chart will look different depending on the agency. Some agencies are full service agencies, which means they do everything, from Strategy to Creative to Media. Other agencies don't have an in-house media group, which means they'll be organized a little differently. At smaller shops, everyone may have to take on the role of Planner/Strategist, because there may not even be a Planning department to begin with.

If you do end up working as a Planner at a large or medium-sized agency, these are the people you'll be working with on a regular basis:

ACCOUNT MANAGERS

Account Managers are the central nervous system of the agency. They're responsible for making sure the accounts they manage are profitable and that the Clients they work with on a daily basis are happy. That means they represent the voice of the Client and the voice of the agency simultaneously. So when you, as a Planner, discover an inconvenient truth about the Clients' business model or the direction consumers are heading, Account Managers may try to soften that truth so as not to offend the Client. That's also why Account Managers are often reputed to be "more Client than Client." That said, the very best Account Managers are highly strategic and can be a Planner's greatest ally. Since they're in touch with Clients so often, they can help you navigate the minefield of Clients' dislikes and idiosyncracies, which will help you immensely when it comes time to sell your strategy. If you routinely provide Account Managers with interesting insights that make them look smarter in front of Clients, they'll make sure you're in the room for high profile meetings.

OTHER ACCOUNT PLANNERS

The way Account Planning departments are staffed, a lot of times you end up working like an independent contractor, which means you don't interact a whole lot with other Planners unless they pull you in on a project or you pull them in on one of yours. So the best thing you can do when you have a little down time is to pay a visit to your fellow Planners and see what they're working on, ask if you can help out and learn how they think. The more exposure you have to more accounts, the more your own thinking and storytelling skills will improve.

MEDIA PLANNERS

If you work at a full service ad agency, that means you'll have a media department. Even if you don't, and the media business is run by another agency, you'll still want to build relationships with the Media Planners as well.

Media, strategy and creative go hand in hand and the media team has access to all sorts of robust databases like Simmons and MRI, which can help with consumer profiles. Also, if you make friends with the media folks, they can get you comps on just about any magazine you want, which is vital to your role as a culture hunter.

INTERNAL RESEARCH DEPARTMENT

Even though Planners are responsible for digging through secondary research, some agencies still have enough of a budget to have at least one research librarian on staff. Make friends with them as soon as possible. They have all the passwords to the research databases that the agency subscribes to and they can show you how to navigate each database so you can find answers faster and more effectively. They're also wizards when it comes to finding stats to random Client questions like "How many cans of condensed soup were sold in the U.S. in 1986?" When you're strapped for time or you just don't know where to begin looking for answers on a particular subject, your research librarian can make a world of difference.

INFORMATION ARCHITECTS

Also sometimes referred to as User Experience Architects or UX for short, these folks are becoming increasingly common at agencies, especially on digital-heavy accounts. Similar to Account Planners, Information Architects are interested in creating maps of the consumer decision process so as to build better online and offline experiences. More often than not, they'll be one of your closest allies when selling strategic ideas to Account Managers, Creatives and Clients.

VENDORS

Before you know it, you'll start getting phone calls and e-mails from all sorts of vendors, trying to sell you research services, copytesting services, social media monitoring services and more. Most likely, your department will have an admin with a Rolodex full of research vendors who can help with things like screeners, recruitment, focus group facilities, etc. However, it's always a good idea to keep track of new vendors. That way, when a research opportunity comes up, you can try something new or at the very least drive down the cost by playing one vendor off another.

CLIENTS

You may not have as much day-to-day contact with Clients as Account Managers do, but you will work with a wide range of Clients on any given account, from "junior level" Clients (who have internal Clients or bosses of their own) all the way up to the CMO (Chief Marketing Officer). One thing to keep in mind as a Planner is that not all Clients are created equal. Some Clients have a lot less marketing experience than others, which means every presentation is an opportunity for Client education. To increase the probability that your strategic thinking will see the light of day, you will want to build solid relationships with all of your Clients, but most importantly with those Clients who are in charge of research. That's where you will be able to have some of the biggest impact, adding new questions to quarterly brand trackers and planting the seeds for research projects that could yield poignant consumer truths. At the end of the day, if you can make your Clients look smarter in front of their bosses, they'll carry your message and your strategy all the way to the top.

PART II: HOW AN AD GETS MADE: FROM INSIGHTS TO IDEAS

THE KICKOFF CALL

FINDING INSIGHTS

CREATIVE BRIEFS

SELLING THE IDEA

THE KICKOFF CALL

Here's a typical situation. At around 10 a.m., you get a meeting request in your inbox from an Account Manager about a kickoff call with a Client you've never met, about a project you've never heard of. All you know is that it's a fast moving project and the meeting will take place in a couple hours via conference call. If you're lucky, the meeting request will have a one-line synopsis of the project you'll be working on. Chances are though, it'll just be a meeting request with the subject heading, "New Project Kickoff Call."

As a Planner, this is one of the challenges you'll face on a regular basis. That's because some Clients view their ad agency as the place that produces the ads rather than as a genuine business partner to be included in the decision making process early on. Unfortunately, Clients don't always think about the Planners at the agency who can provide valuable strategic input. They think about the agency as the place that comes up with the creative output. In other words, advertising agencies are typically downstream from where the real decision-making takes place.

That means while you were doing "plannerly" things like reading magazine articles and eMarkter reports about the latest trends in consumer behavior and social media, your Clients were having important meetings back at headquarters, signing off on budgets and making decisions about what their next communications effort or advertising campaign is going to be. It might be a 100 year anniversary video for the annual convention or it might be a new product launch. Either way, the Clients you're about to talk to over the phone have already started talking about what the campaign might look like or who they think the celebrity spokesperson should be.

Your job during that thirty minute kickoff call is to figure out what the project is all about and what questions you need to ask to help make the creative brief that much smarter and more insightful.

Typically, Creatives aren't on the initial kickoff call with the Client. But if the project needs to be turned around in less than 72 hours, you'll probably have a couple of Creatives there as well.

To give you a better senese of what separates Account Managers from Account Planners, here are the most common questions each person brings to the party.

ACCOUNT MANAGER:

→ What are we trying to achieve with this communications effort? What's our goal? Awareness? Traffic? Sales?

→ What have you tried in the past, in terms of communicating with this audience? Has it worked well? What were the results? What do you think could have been done better?

→ What's the time frame for this project? Is there an event or another effort driving this in-market date?

→ What's the budget for this project? Is that budget just for production, or does it also include media?

→ Who within your organization will need to approve the project, and at what stages?

→ What existing assets do you have that we might be able to tap into for this assignment?

→ What mandates or "must haves" do we need to take into consideration? Logos? Specific wording in the call-to-action? Website URL? Social media icons?

→ In what format will we need to deliver the final product? (e.g. dvd, digital file, etc.?)

ACCOUNT PLANNER:

→ Who are we talking to?

→ What do they currently feel, think or do when it comes to our brand or our product? Why do they feel that way? What's causing that perception or that behavior? Do they feel that way about the entire category or just about us?

→ What do we want them to feel, think or do as a result of our messaging/communications?

→ What else do we know about them that can help us? Do you have any additional primary research about your best customers or your target customers that we can look at (e.g. segmentation studies, demographics/ psychographic profiles, verbatims from ethnographies, focus groups, man-on-the-street interviews, loyalty program stats, etc.)?

→ What's the one thing you want the audience to walk away with as a result of seeing this piece of communications?

→ What else is happening in the category? Anything new or interesting?

→ What are your closest competitors doing?

→ Do we have any new news to share in this communications effort? (Is there anything special about what we're offering? If there's nothing new to say or if it's a "me too" offering, then this is where Planning really comes into play, because as a Planner you're going to have to find something interesting in the culture, the category or in the attitudes and perceptions of the target consumers to help make the message relevant and stand out.)

→ What does success look like? (This ties back in with the goal, but is more focused on specific metrics.)

Of course, there is no cut and dry division of responsibility when it comes to asking these kinds of questions. There are plenty of strategically minded Account Managers out there and some very creative Planners. The good news is, if you're on a team where everyone is thinking strategically and creatively, you're bound to make great work, even if you're on a 72-hour deadline.

FINDING INSIGHTS

When most people think of Planners, they think of one word: insights. Our job is to look at the world with a fresh set of eyes and see things that no one else has noticed before. The question is, how do we get those insights? What's the secret? Contrary to popular belief, there is not a mythical tree inside our offices from which we pluck insights on a daily basis. Also contrary to popular belief, meaningful consumer insights are not usually found inside most Client presentations, which are usually filled with all sorts of colorful charts and reams of sales data.

So where do we get these amazing insights from? An easy place to start whenever you're confronted with a communications challenge is to look more closely at the four Cs.

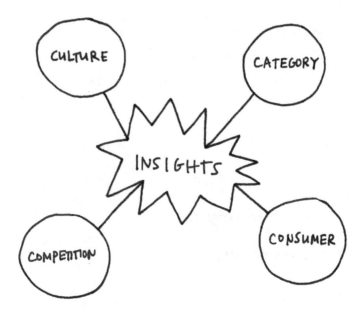

This is why most Planners are insatiable consumers of pop culture. Movies, music, concerts, sporting events, bars, restaurants, museums – you name it – Planners like to be in the thick of it, notebooks and cameras in hand, participating and observing at the same time.

Planners are also voracious readers of newspapers, magazines, industry reports, blogs, in-store promotional displays, the backs of cereal boxes – anything we can get our eyeballs on.

It's this constant cross-pollinating of high culture, low culture and pop culture that gives us our unique perspective on the issues as well as plenty of metaphors with which to describe things.

Beyond personal experience and secondary sources, there are also a number of methods and research tools that we routinely use to see the world from the eyes of specific consumers, including:

→ Focus Groups

→ Consumer Ethnographies

→ Stakeholder Interviews

→ Customer Intercepts

→ Surveys/Questionnaires

→ Social Media Monitoring

→ Data Mining

Ultimately, the best insights come from being out in the world. If you really want to discover poignant human truths, you have to step away from the computer and be around other human beings for a while. You have to talk to them. You have to watch them in context. You have to take notes (or better yet take video). And perhaps most importantly, you have to keep asking yourself why they're doing whatever it is they're doing. People are complex, emotional and highly irrational. Often, they'll tell you only what they think you want to hear. Your job as a Planner is to find ways around their well-intentioned white lies and figure out what they really think about the situation at hand, or what they would really do if you gave them $100 or $1,000 to spend on anything they wanted.

One hour spent talking to or observing another human being in the right context will often give you more insight than one month spent behind a computer monitor, looking at spreadsheets or industry reports.

THE REAL VALUE
THAT YOU BRING
AS A PLANNER
IS IN PROVIDING
A UNIQUE POINT
OF VIEW, WHICH
USUALLY MEANS
FINDING SOURCES
OF INFORMATION
THAT NO ONE ELSE
IS LOOKING AT.

FOCUS GROUPS

Among the general public, focus groups are perhaps the most well-known method for gleaning insights from consumers. You see them all the time in movies and television shows. The one way mirror. A bunch of guys in suits standing behind that one-way mirror. And a group of people sitting in a nondescript room being asked a bunch of questions about their favorite lipstick or the kind of shampoo they use and why.

Times have changed. And focus groups, while still relatively popular, are by no means the only way Planners get insights. That said, if your Clients say they want to do focus groups, here are a few basics to get you started and stay on top of what's going on.

What are your objectives?

What is it you really want to know? Focus groups are an opportunity to ask the kinds of questions that don't get asked in industry reports. They're an opportunity to let people answer open-ended questions so that you can get a fresh perspective on the situation at hand and pick up a few insights in the process.

How many people per focus group?

There are a few options here. One-on-one. Pairs. Small groups (3-6 people). And larger groups (7-10 people). Obviously, one-on-one lets you go deeper, but if the respondent doesn't feel at ease, then the session will end up looking and feeling more like an interrogation. Pairs can be very revealing, especially if you talk to husbands and wives or best friends, because they're usually much more comfortable with each other and are more likely to talk freely. Small groups can be a bit more challenging because respondents won't know each other, which means everyone will have their guard up. However, if you have a good moderator and a good discussion guide, small groups can also be very rewarding and yield a lot of insights. In rare cases, because of research budgets or timing, you may end up doing large focus groups with 7-10 people, but it's not ideal, because what usually ends up happening is that not everyone gets a chance to talk or each person talks very briefly and you never get on a roll.

If you're working on a national brand and budgets allow, you'll probably want to do focus groups in at least 3-4 different markets (northeast, south, west coast, midwest).

Developing a Screener

Unfortunately, you can't just ask anyone to be part of your focus group. I know. It's not nice, but that's just the way it is. You need to find people who have the same characteristics as the customers you're trying to reach. So to do that, you have to develop a screener, which screens out the people you don't want.

In many cases, the Client's internal research department will develop the screener themselves , but if you build solid relationships with them, chances are they'll ask you to give it a once over and see if there's anything that you'd like to add. Once the screener is done, the Client will most likely hire a third party vendor to do the necessary recruiting to find the right respondents.

Focus Group Facilities

You have to have your focus group somewhere, right? Most of the time, that means you'll be going to a focus group facility, which are those non-descript rooms I mentioned earlier. The problem with focus group facilities is that they're neutral, artificial environments. It's a plain room inside of a plain building with a plain conference table and a bunch of plain chairs, not to mention that giant one-way mirror. It doesn't exactly put people at ease. However, the real benefit of a focus group facility is that it's a controlled environment. Video cameras, microphones and the back room are already set up, so it's pretty much just plug and play.

However, focus groups don't always have to be in a neutral facility. It is possible to do focus groups inside a person's home, where the benefit, of course, is that it's a more relaxed environment. The problem is that it's not a controlled environment, which means you may have all sorts of external noises that distract your respondents and mess up your audio. Plus, you can only have a limited number of people (e.g. videographer, moderator, planner, account manager) before you start to lose that whole "relaxed" and "informal" feeling.

The Moderator

The moderator is the most important part of a focus group session. He or she sets the pace, controls the tempo, gets people to feel at ease, and keeps things on topic. Depending on the circumstances, you may end up moderating a focus group or two, but chances are, if you're in a big agency, the Client's research department will set everything up and hire a moderator. That means you, too, will be an observer in the back room with the the rest of the Clients, trying to avoid the ever-distracting buffet table with its endless array of cheese, crackers, and sweets.

The Discussion Guide

The discussion guide is what the moderator uses to stay on topic during the focus group. Ultimately, though, it's just a guide. Great moderators have an intuitive sense for when people are starting to open up, and they have all sorts of clever ways for getting people to reveal even more. Watching a great moderator is like watching a great journalist at work. They get people to say things that a lesser moderator could not. Here's a quick example of a discussion guide on the subject of volunteering:

Warm up questions [5-10 minutes]

→ What comes to mind when I say the word volunteering?

→ What comes to mind when I say the phrase community service?

→ What's the difference, in your opinion, between these two ideas?

Detailed story-telling on most recent volunteering opportunity. [30 minutes]

Think about your most recent experience in which you spent some time participating in a local volunteer opportunity.

→ Tell me about this situation like you're telling a story.

→ Take a few minutes to describe what you did, how you got involved with it, why you decided to do it, etc.

Now I'm going to ask some more specific questions about this situation.

→ What specifically triggered your desire to volunteer?

→ What organization were you involved with, if any? What did you do?

→ How did you first learn about this opportunity?

→ What triggered your interest in giving your time to this specific opportunity?

→ Who specificially had an influence on you for getting involved in this opportunity? At what points did they play a role? How did they influence you?

Second Story [15 minutes]

Now I want you to think about another experience in which you volunteered your time. Think specifically of a time where you actively sought out the opportunity, rather than responding to being asked by someone.

→ Like before, take a few minutes to describe what you did, how you got involved with it, why you decided to do it, etc.

→ How was that experience different from your most recent experience? Think particularly in terms of how you got involved in it and decided to do it.

Third Story [15 minutes]

Now I want you to think about one more experience. This time think about the volunteer or service opportunity that has been your least favorite for one reason or another.

→ Take a few minutes to describe what you did, how you got involved with it, why you decided to do it, how you felt about it, etc.

→ How was this experience different from the others you've described? Think particularly in terms of how you got involved in it and decided to do it.

The real challenge with focus groups and discussion guides is figuring out how much time you'll need for each section of the conversation. The clock is always ticking, which means you have a limited amount of time to ask your most insightful questions. If you spend too much time on the warm-up questions, you won't have enough time to get to the real meat of the conversation. However, if you don't make your respondents feel at ease right away, then the conversation may feel stilted and people will never tell you what it is they're really thinking. That's where the art of moderating comes into play.

Ultimately, focus groups can be a lot of fun. And if they're done well, they can yield some amazing insights, which you can then confirm or refine through quantitative research. The trick to a successful focus group (and all research for that matter) is figuring out what it is you really want to know and then making sure you work closely with the parties involved (namely the Client's research department and the moderator) so that you can get past the obvious answers and ask the kinds of questions that most people would never think to ask.

ETHNOGRAPHIES

It's really no surprise, but there's a big difference between what people say they do and what they actually do. In focus groups, people are only allowed to tell you what they *would* do. In ethnographies, you get to see what they *really* do. It's about as close as you can get to walking a mile in another person's shoes. Sometimes, the results can be both amusing and insightful, like when a married couple who claim to be deeply concerned about the environment have a hybrid parked next to an SUV in their garage, and leave the lights on in every room, blazing at full power. Or when a diabetic pours two tablespoons of sugar into his coffee after explaining why he refuses jelly for his toast.

Ethnographies, or "ethnos" for short, allow you to see people in the context of their own environment, (as opposed to a focus group facility), which means they tend to be more comfortable, allowing you to see the gaps between their stories and the way they actually behave. Whereas focus groups can be pushed this way or that by more vocal or insistent participants, one-to-one ethnographies can be more like an eight hour confessional. After the first couple hours, people forget about the camera and let their guards down, sharing things they might not otherwise share in a group context. Like the woman in a study about incontinence products who confessed to the videographer that she'd never asked her husband how he felt about her condition. "Maybe I don't want to hear the answer to that," she said. It's intimate moments like that which can lead to powerful insights.

And while you may catch a glimpse of certain insights as you go from city to city, listening to people talk about their favorite shoes and video taping them as they try on their

18th pair, it's when you get back to the office and analyze the 50-100 hours of footage that you really start to see all the subtleties, which is when you'll have your most powerful "aha!" moments.

WHEN SHOULD YOU DO AN ETHNOGRAPHY VS. A FOCUS GROUP?

FOCUS GROUPS ARE IDEAL WHEN:	ETHNOGRAPHIES ARE IDEAL WHEN:
You don't have a lot of time	You have more time (around 2 - 6 months)
You don't have a lot of money	You have more money
You want to ask several people a set of specific questions	You want to get a deeper understanding of people's motivations
You don't mind if the answers are out of context	You want to see people's behavior in context.

As an Account Planner, the biggest challenge with ethnographies is selling the idea to the Client in the first place. Here's why. First, a typical ethnography costs anywhere from $50K - $100K. That's because you usually need to recruit anywhere from 6 to 10 people, with each person getting paid as much as $500. Plus, it costs a lot of money to pay for the entire entourage (e.g. videographer, ethnographer, etc.) to go to all those cities where the respondents are located. Second, the entire process for an average study can take anywhere from 4-8 weeks.

Since Clients tend to think about quarterly profits, studies that take an entire quarter to execute are usually frowned upon. Finally, after all is said and done, the results you get at the end of this fascinating process are only qualitative, meaning they're not "statistically significant," which means a lot of Clients may not be willing to bet their next $10 million campaign on a handful of verbatims and a couple of interesting insights, no matter how snazzy your five minute ethnographic video may be.

If you are able to sell your Clients on an ethnography, here are a couple of basic strategies to keep in mind:

→ **Get people to do the activity rather than just tell you about it.** Remember, if all you wanted were stories, you could have just as easily done a focus group. The beauty of doing an ethnography is that you can see how people really go through the process as they describe it to you. Sometimes, the insights can come from the disparity between their words and their actions. Other times, the insights will come from the description they give you as they tell you their motivations for doing things a certain way.

→ **Take pictures and videos of the surroundings.** Ethnographies are a lot like detective work. People tend to leave clues lying around without realizing it. In many cases, you may not immediately pick up on those clues while you're asking them questions or listening to their stories. That's why it's important to take pictures and videos of everything around you, so you can go back and analyze the evidence after the fact.

ONE MORE THING:

Depending on the agency and/or the Client, your ethnographic research may end up being outsourced to a third party vendor. That's because Planners typically have too many other assignments to be away from the agency for that long.

STAKEHOLDER INTERVIEWS

Even though Planners are often described as "the voice of the consumer," a big part of a Planner's job is getting to know how the Client's business operates. That means conducting stakeholder interviews inside Client headquarters. Stakeholders can be everyone from the CMO to the product development team, all the way to the janitor. Understanding a Client's internal culture is especially important, not only for political purposes when you're giving presentations, but so that you can effectively help the Client create and communicate their brand's core identity to everyone else in the organization as quickly and concisely as possible.

Every stakeholder interview is a little different depending on the assignment and the respondent, but here are a few classic questions to help you get started:

→ Tell me about your time here at X brand. What's it like working here? What's changed since you've been here? How long have you worked here?

→ Let's talk about X brand and its people. What are the types of people who work here? How would you describe them? What type of person does X brand look to hire? What are the kinds of people who succeed here?

→ Describe for me what X brand is like on its best day. What makes for a great day at X brand? What about on its worst day? What are some of the things that get in the way of making every day a great day at X brand?

→ What does X brand do best?

→ What could X brand do better?

→ What do you think makes X brand unique? How is it better than the competition?

→ What do you think our customers get from our brand that they can't get anywhere else? What is our commitment to them?

→ What do you think this brand will stand for in the future?

→ How would you improve this brand? How do you think our customers could help improve our brand?

And here are a few additional questions, using what's known as "projective techniques," to let your respondents be more imaginative and have a little more fun:

If this brand were a person...

→ How would you describe him (or her)?

→ What do you think he likes to do for fun?

→ What does he do on weekends?

→ How would you describe his friends?

→ What kind of party would he throw?

→ If he went on vacation what kind of vacation would he go on?

CUSTOMER INTERCEPTS

For many brands, especially retail brands, customer intercepts are a convenient middle-ground between focus groups and ethnographies. Instead of following certain customers around for several days or even weeks, you approach them in the store, right outside the store, or somewhere on the sidewalk, and talk to them for a few minutes. It's a chance to get a quick read on people's thoughts and feelings on a particular subject in context rather than in a focus group room.

The most important thing to remember is that with customer intercepts, time is of the essence. That's because most people are either in a hurry or they're extremely focused on what it is they're buying, which means they're not usually all that interested in stopping to talk to a complete stranger who claims to be a market researcher. In most cases, you have less than thirty seconds to tell them who you are, who you're with, what you're doing, and what you can give them in return for just 5-7 minutes of their time. Most of the time, people will say "no thanks" or wave you off even before you can tell them your name, so it's important that you have a thick skin and are comfortable with rejection.

As with all research, the same basic parameters apply. Who do you want to talk to, what is it you really want to know, and what are the best questions you can ask in that five minute window in order to get the insights you're looking for? Once you have identified those key elements, here are some additional things you can do to make your customer intercepts more successful.

Make sure the manager knows you're coming

As you can imagine, store managers can get a little crazy if they see someone they don't know interviewing one of their customers, either in-store or in the parking lot. Are you with the competition? Are you doing some kind of documentary? Who gave you permission to be on their property and harass their customers? So before you approach anyone for an interview, make sure you've gotten in touch with the manager a couple of days in advance and introduce yourself when you arrive. That way, the manager can tell all the other employees that you're legit, which means you won't get chased off the property with a baseball bat.

Bring a buddy

Male/Female combinations typically work best. That's because, as you can probably imagine, two men approaching a woman in the parking lot outside a store can be more than a little intimidating. Having at least one woman on your team can help reduce that tension and put your respondents more at ease.

Carry a clipboard

The clipboard is mainly just a prop. It signals to people as you're walking toward them that you're doing some kind of official research. Plus, you never know what kinds of questions you'll want to jot down on the fly while the person is talking.

Bring a video camera

It's always good to get video footage of consumers talking. That way, if you get some great sound bytes, you can edit them together in a short video that can be shared with the Client and/or the Creative team. However, video cameras have a tendency to make people nervous. So don't come running toward your respondent with the camera pulled out like you're with the paparazzi. Make your introductions first. Then tell them what you're doing and have your colleague casually pull out the video camera as you ask the customer if you can record their responses for note-taking purposes only. Many people will be very agreeable until they see the video camera, so be prepared to tell them a couple of times that it's just for note-taking purposes and that their responses will not end up on YouTube or on television. This is also where having a partner can come in handy, since he/she can be the videographer, allowing you and the respondent to focus more on the conversation.

Offer customers something for their time

As early as you can, tell them you'd like to give them something in exchange for their time. You might even want to introduce yourself by saying, "How would you like a $10 gift card for just five minutes of your time?" Whatever your technique and whatever it is the Client has provided you with (coupons, free product samples, gift cards, etc.), just make sure that the customer understands that you'd like to give them something in exchange for their time. Also, tell them, just as you would in a focus group, that their honest and candid feedback will ultimately help the business do a better job of meeting their needs.

The one major drawback with customer intercepts as a research technique is that it involves something called "convenient sampling", which typically means you're dealing with a small sample size, so the results you get may not be true across regions or applicable to all demographics. However, when you have less than a week to turn a brief around and there's nothing terribly insightful coming from your secondary sources, then customer intercepts are a great way to uncover some interesting insights, which will make your Creatives very, very happy.

SURVEYS/QUESTIONNAIRES

It's important to remember that when people wake up in the morning, they don't think to themselves, "I can't wait to take a survey today about shampoo or toilet bowl cleaner or my personal experience with quitting smoking!" Even if they get a "reward" for taking the survey, it's not exactly something most people enjoy doing.

A survey or questionnaire can be as short or as long as you want it to be. It all depends on what it is you want to know.

One thing to keep in mind when designing your survey – it's not as easy as scribbling down a handful of questions and sending them to everyone you know. Unlike focus groups, where you can ask someone for additional clarity on what they meant by a particular answer, you don't have that luxury with questionnaires. With quantitative questionnaires, you're likely reaching out to hundreds if not thousands of people, which means the questionnaire needs to be as buttoned up as possible. If the data is skewed because of a poorly worded question or because people got confused and decided to abandon the questionnaire, you probably won't get the chance to field another survey to an additional thousand respondents to make it right.

That's why great survey design is both an art and a science. There are a lot of variables that can skew your results, so you have to be mindful of a wide variety of factors, including the big three: order bias, question phrasing and survey length.

ORDER BIAS

The order of your questions and the multiple choice answers that follow are important. To avoid order bias, always make sure to randomize the order in which responses are displayed.

QUESTION PHRASING

How a question is phrased can lead to dramatically different answers. For example, in a January 2003 Pew Research survey, when people were asked whether they would: "favor or oppose taking military action in Iraq to end Saddam Hussein's rule," 68% said they favored military action while 25% said they opposed military action. However, when asked whether they would "favor or oppose taking military action in Iraq to end Saddam Hussein's rule even if it meant that U.S. forces might suffer thousands of casualties," responses were dramatically different; only 43% said they favored military action while 48% said they opposed it.

So take your time and really think through the wording of every question. Put yourself in the shoes of the person answering it. Imagine all the ways that they could misinterpret the question or give you a response that would be less than useful.

SURVEY LENGTH

If your survey is too long, respondents will experience something called "survey fatigue" and they'll start clicking on the first thing they see to get through the survey as fast as possible. If you feel like your survey is getting too long, double check your objectives. Maybe you have too many. Maybe one survey isn't enough to find out all the information you're looking for.

No matter how short or long your survey is though, there's ultimately just one question you have to ask yourself. "Will the answers to these questions tell me something I don't already know?" If the answer is yes, great! If the answer is no, keep working on your survey.

SOCIAL MEDIA MONITORING

In the past few years, social media monitoring tools like Radian6, Collective Intellect, Spredfast and Crimson Hexagon (among many others) have given Planners another way to listen to conversations beyond the focus group room. Now we can track everything that's being said on Twitter, Facebook, YouTube, blogs, and a host of other sites where consumers are sharing their thoughts with the brand and with each other.

The great thing about these tools is that they allow you to keep close tabs on a particular campaign or discover an emerging trend in real time, which means you have the potential to find insights and put them to use in a matter of days, as opposed to weeks or even months with more traditional research methods. The challenge with these tools, however, is that you have to calibrate them very, very carefully, which means you have to be crystal clear on what your objectives are and what exactly it is you want to listen for. Unlike a focus group, there is no moderator or discussion guide. It's just a fire hose of individual comments and conversations and it's your job to figure out which filters to put on the conversation to make it more manageable and find something of value. Even if you do get everything calibrated just right, it's easy to get sucked down the rabbit hole of word clouds, sentiment analysis, influencer scores and follower counts. Plus, it's not like you set it up once and you're done. With social media monitoring tools, you have to constantly refine your filters and analyze new conversations in an effort to uncover more meaningful insights. As a result, these tools can be extremely labor intensive, which means there's an opportunity cost. Time. How much time does it take to get to an actionable insight? Even though there's great potential to discover insights among the hundreds of thousands of conversations happening in real time, it's important to note that you can also discover powerful consumer insights while sitting in a coffee shop or walking through a mall.

Most agencies and Clients are still figuring out how best to use these tools and how to staff for them as well. As a Planner, you should definitely know how these tools work, but always remember, your greatest contribution will be the way you approach the conversation, the assumptions you make and the questions you ask. That's why social media monitoring can never be a substitute for the discipline of Planning. The tools we use, whether they're digital or analog, are only as effective as the people who use them.

DATA MINING

As more and more devices and touchpoints go digital, there's an opportunity to find insights in the "data footprints" that customers leave behind during their decision making process. From mobile phones to desktop banners to search engine traffic , we live in an era of big data, with trillions of bytes streaming into servers every second. That's why big brands and ad agencies are developing data analytics teams, to make sense of all that data and do something useful with it, for both the brand and the consumer.

Here are a couple of examples of how crunching the numbers and leveraging data have helped different businesses find previously hidden insights, which has, in turn, improved the customer's experience.

EXAMPLE #1: TROUBLE IN THE ER

A few years ago, a hospital in Washington D.C. noticed that a large number of patients were returning to the ER within a few weeks of being discharged. To find answers, the hospital dug into the data, analyzing more than 300,000 ER visits, looking for patterns among 25,000 different variables, including the patients' medications, vital signs and doctors. In the thicket of all that data, they discovered two key correlations. First, if the length of the patient's original stay was more than 14 hours, the patient was likely to return. Second, if there was any mention of the word "fluid" on the patient's medical chart, it significantly increased the likelihood of readmission.

By analyzing hospital data like this, the hospital is now able to produce a more accurate readmissions forecast for each patient, which means better care for more patients, and hundreds of millions of dollars in savings.[1]

EXAMPLE #2: THESE EARRINGS WOULD GO GREAT WITH THAT DRESS!

When Neiman Marcus wanted to take their renowned customer service to the next level, data mining helped by providing them with a powerful insight: customers who shop with the same associate three times spend almost ten times more than those who go to a random sales clerk. The result: the Neiman Marcus Service App, which allows customers to see which associates are on the floor as soon as they walk into the store. For Neiman Marcus Associates, the app gives them a fuller picture of each customers' shopping history, both offline and

online, so that the associate has a better understanding of the customers' preferences and can offer relevant items that might complement previous purchases, such as a pair of earrings to go with a cocktail dress that was recently bought online.[2]

EXAMPLE #3: EVERY VOTE COUNTS

Political campaigns have also turned to data mining to help get out the vote and increase donation levels. In a recent election in the U.S., campaign managers cobbled together voter profiles using information from Facebook, Twitter, and other publicly available sources, which allowed them to offer hyper-focused messaging on specific issues. With their custom built algorithms and data analytics teams, they were able to learn that certain voters only opened campaign e-mails about veterans' issues and never opened e-mails about jobs. That insight led the campaign team to send more e-mails about veterans issues to those specific constituents throughout the campaign, increasing open rates and greater participation at the polls.[3]

THE BOTTOM LINE

Insights that come from data mining can impact the business well beyond marketing. As a Planner, you probably won't be sifting through the data on a daily basis, but you will have to ask for certain kinds of data, so it's important that you build a good relationship with the Clients who own the data in the first place. When it comes to selling the strategy, it helps if you can back up your insights with data points from the Client's own databases. And finally, when Creatives ask you questions like, "How do people use their mobile devices at point of purchase for a particular product?" you'll become indispensable to them if you have that data in your back pocket.

---

[1] Manjoo, Farhad. "Big Changes Are Ahead For The Health Care Industry, Courtesy Of Big Data." Fast Company, 18 June 2012.

[2] Associated Press. "Neiman Marcus Testing IPhone App." Today.com. NBC News, 2 Mar. 2012.

[3] McGregor, Richard. "Inside Obama's HQ." Financial Times, 14 Sept. 2012.

THE CREATIVE BRIEF IS A DOCUMENT.

THE CREATIVE *BRIEFING* IS AN ART FORM.

CREATIVE BRIEFS & CREATIVE BRIEFING

The creative brief is really just the beginning of a conversation between Creatives and Planners. Some Creatives like to have a hand in developing the creative brief. Others don't want to see anything until you've nailed down an insight. Either way, your brief should be insightful, inspiring and grounded in a consumer truth. If the creative idea is rooted in a strong strategic idea, the campaign is more likely to become culturally infectious and last for a long time.

Of course, every agency works hard on developing a creative brief that looks a certain way, so in reality there is no such thing as a "standard" brief. Creative briefs come in all shapes and sizes. However, there are a few key questions that you'll see on just about every brief, including:

→ What's the situation and why are we communicating?

→ What's the business objective?

→ What's the communications objective?

→ Who are we talking to? (a.k.a. who's the target?)

→ What do they currently feel/think/do and why?

→ What do we want them to feel/think/do?

→ What's the ONE thing we need to say to get them to feel/ think/do that?

→ What tone should we take?

→ How are we going to measure success? Sales? Web traffic? Likes/Followers? Social media engagement?

Some agencies have developed other questions that can yield additional insights and give Creatives "other ways in" to solving the communications challenge.

→ What territory are we trying to own for the brand?

→ What do we know about the brand that could help us start a dialogue between the brand and our target and/or within the popular culture in general?

→ What else do we know about our target that can help us? What's the consumer or category insight that we can tap into in a creative way? What's the cultural tension that we might be able to take advantage of?

Depending on the assignment, you may end up briefing a team that's never worked on the business before, which means they know nothing about the brand and they're starting off from scratch. That's why the creative briefing is the most precarious stage in the process between Planners and

Creatives. If it's done poorly, the work suffers. If it's done well, it's the moment where your words and insights leap off the page and start doing cartwheels in the minds of Creatives.

For a briefing to be engaging and inspiring, it needs to be more than just you handing out copies of the brief and reading it out loud like a student in a 10th grade English class. It needs to be a collaborative environment where Creatives begin brainstorming without even realizing it.

Of course, some Creatives will want to skip past the other parts of the brief and get straight to the consumer insight. Your job as a Planner is to turn the brief into a compelling story so that the Creatives don't want to skip ahead.

To do that, here are a few tricks for holding your Creative team's attention:

BRIEF WITH ENTHUSIASM

If you treat the assignment like it's small potatoes or a waste of time, it'll rub off on them. Remember, your attitude affects theirs.

CONTROL THE TEMPO

In addition to handing out copies of the brief, bring a PowerPoint version and a projector. Put each section of the brief on its own dedicated slide.

CREATE A SITUATION ROOM
(A.K.A. A "WAR" ROOM)

Before the briefing begins, work with an assistant
account executive or an intern to set up the room with
as much category/competitive imagery as you can find.
Make the briefing into an immersive experience. If
time and resources don't allow you to prep the room
beforehand, make sure Creatives have access to all the
files for later viewing.

Ultimately, a great brief (and briefing) should help Creatives
see the problem, the consumer, or the category in a new
way. Once you're done with the briefing, make sure
Creatives know how they can get a hold of you. If they don't
call or write, don't take offense. Some Creatives are more
introverted than others. Just swing by their offices and
see if they want to chat. Ask them if there's anything else
you can do to help them out. Ask them if there's anything
else they want to know about the consumer. The more
you collaborate, the more you'll be able to keep the work
on strategy and the easier it will be to sell the work to the
Account Management team as well as the Client.

THE STRATEGIC
IDEA IS WHAT
WE NEED TO SAY.

THE CREATIVE
IDEA IS HOW
WE'RE GOING
TO SAY IT.

WHAT IS A CULTURAL TENSION?

David Ogilvy pioneered the idea of tapping into cultural tensions. Here's how it's defined on Ogilvy's website:

> *The Cultural Tension is not simply an identification of a consumer need, it is much more than that. It is an articulation of something that is wrong with the world that needs changing, and that is addressable by the brand in question... It is about what the brand is like when it is at its best.*

The way I like to think of it is that cultural tensions are the result of two major societal trends pulling in opposite directions. It's like a tug of war with the brand in the middle, playing referee. If the brand plays it right, the brand gets all the attention. Here are a few examples:

DOVE

In 2003, Dove tapped into the cultural tension inherent in society's mixed messages about beauty. On the one side, there were countless mass media images celebrating hypersexualized women, sculpted to a point of perfection. On the other side, there was growing frustration among women who said that such images were impossible to live up to. The cultural tension: "be like these models" vs. "just be yourself." Dove's solution: "The Campaign for Real Beauty." The big idea focused on getting people to talk about what real beauty meant to them and challenging mass media stereotypes in the process.

NESTLE'S CHOCOLATE DRINK MILO

In 2007, Nestle unearthed a cultural tension in Malaysia between work and play. They noticed that in fast-growing economies like Malaysia, there was increased pressure on children to focus on academic work, which meant children were discouraged from playing sports. Nestle's solution: "Supplying the fuel for kids to succeed." The big idea was centered around the belief that play is the essential work of childhood and that kids learn by playing.

LEVI'S "GO FORTH" CAMPAIGN

In 2009, Levi leveraged a cultural tension involving the "pioneer spirit," combining a heritage of hard work and youthful entrepreneurialism against a backdrop of American uncertainty in the face of economic strife and global competition. The campaign idea, which went global in 2012, never talks about Levi's unique stitching patterns or how durable its products are, but instead focuses on the entrepreneurial aspirations of young people everywhere.

SELLING THE IDEA

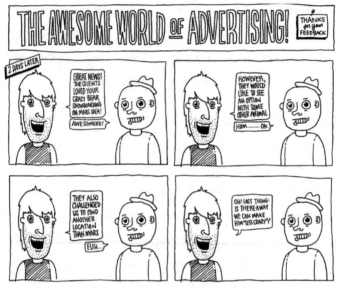

Courtesy of The Awesome World of Advertising

Creatives love coming up with ideas. And like all artists, what they want more than anything else is to get their ideas out into the world. To do that though, they have to sell their ideas internally. To the Executive Creative Director. To the Account Management team. And, of course, to the Client. That's where you come in. If Creatives see you as their partner and if they believe that you want to sell their work as much as they do, then they're more likely to invite you into the creative process early on, which will allow you to influence the work and keep it on track from a strategic perspective.

Of course, how you do this is a delicate dance. If you say something in the wrong way, no matter how good your intention, feelings will be hurt, trust will evaporate, and you'll be left out in the cold with the rest of the Account Management team, waiting to see the work for the first time at the first internal review.

To become the Creatives' ally, and to be seen as an indispensable part of the creative process, here are a few basic tips to keep in mind when reviewing creative work:

→ Always start the review by highlighting the elements of the work that you really like, explaining why those elements are particularly strong from a strategic standpoint.

→ Always frame your talking points from the consumer's perspective. Use consumer research as your support. That way, the critique isn't coming from you. It's coming from what you know about the consumer.

→ Let Creatives know about certain "hot button" issues that the Client has previously mentioned – e.g. certain words, phrases, images, or ideas that Clients don't like or that will cause a firestorm internally. Creatives hate being told what to do, so don't tell them not to use those words, phrases, etc. Just let them know that they should "keep these things in mind."

→ If they haven't already done so, help Creatives organize their ideas into specific territories or "buckets." When it comes time to present to Clients, it will allow the Clients to focus on one idea at a time, while also helping them see the difference between each territory.

→ Never interrupt the description of the creative idea. Wait until the end of the Creative presentation (or at the very least, until the end of each creative idea) to share your feedback. Don't nit-pick the idea at a number of different places or ask dozens of questions. This will be seen as an assault. Organize your thoughts on paper so that you have a few specific talking points that are, as mentioned before, grounded in consumer research. (Note: Organizing your thoughts on the fly is a critical skill that comes with time.)

Of course, there are some Creatives who, for years, have made plenty of great, award-winning work without a Planner's input. This means they may resent the idea of having a Planner tell them what the strategy should be. If that's the case, it may take a little longer to earn their trust and make them realize you're an ally. Just remember to stay enthusiastic about the work and keep bringing them useful information in bite-sized chunks about the target or the category. Find ways to show them you're on the same team, even if that means doing something simple, like getting them a cup of coffee. The core of any relationship is trust. If Creatives feel they can trust you, if they believe you can help them achieve their goal of selling the work, they'll see to it that you'll always have a seat at the table.

Depending on the assignment, the timeline and the teams you're working with, you'll typically have anywhere from one to three internal reviews before you share the work with the Client. And while you should be working hand-in-hand with the Creatives throughout the process, each review is an opportunity for everyone to ask questions, challenge assumptions and offer suggestions, making the work more "buttoned up" with each iteration, so that when it comes time to sell the varying ideas to the Client, the presentation is as tight and professional as it can be.

The Creative presentation is, by and large, the Creatives' show, and it is a carefully choreographed performance. The Account Director usually kicks things

off, the Planner may remind everyone about the agreed upon strategic direction, but the Creatives do most of the talking. That said, as the Account Planner, you'll want to be prepared for potential questions that may come up about how the work relates to the insight/strategy. If you've been working with the Creatives the entire time, they should be able to answer the Client's questions themselves, but since it's your job to know the consumer better than anyone else, it's also an opportunity for you to pepper in some bite-sized insights that can connect the dots between the strategic idea and the creative execution. Again, make sure you always frame your answers from the perspective of the consumer and keep your comments grounded in research.

If all goes well, the Client will love the ideas presented and will have a hard time choosing, because they're all so good. If that's the case, the Client will inevitably ask the entire team, "Which campaign is your favorite?" As a team, you should always be prepared to answer that question, so it's best to make sure you talk about it beforehand.

PART III: ORGANIZED CHAOS (A.K.A. THE DAY-TO-DAY LIFE OF A PLANNER)

CONCEPT TESTING

COPY TESTING

WHITE PAPERS

BRAINSTORMING

NEW BUSINESS

POSITIONING

BRAND ARCHITECTURE

SEGMENTATION STUDIES

DEVELOPING PERSONAS

CONSUMER DECISION PROCESS MAPS

PRO BONO WORK

AWARD SHOWS

CONCEPT TESTING

Let's say your Client has a new product they want to launch. Before you start making ads, you need to figure out which value proposition or "concept" resonates most with consumers. That's why you do concept testing.

For example, let's say you're trying to figure out what consumers value most when it comes to potato chips. Is it crunch, texture, flavor, color, or something else? It's important to know because that information is going to influence what goes front and center in the ads, on the packaging, and just about everywhere else.

Or, let's say you're trying to figure out what's most important to consumers when it's time to choose a particular retail store to buy a new refrigerator. Obviously, price is a given, but what else will get the vast majority of customers to choose your retail business over someone else's? Is it selection, customer service, free delivery, warranty, maintenance, or something else? Chances are, it's a combination of all these things, but you have to figure which one (or two) concepts consumers value most.

Once you and the client decide which concepts you're going to test, you need to keep the concept statements as straightforward as possible. That means you need to use plain language.

For example, let's say your Client is a home improvement retailer who wants to get more customers to schedule in-home consultations for installation jobs. Here are some examples of the kinds of concept statements a consumer might read.

Expert Advice

When it comes to a project this big, you're not exactly sure what makes one product better than the next, or what you should even be looking for. **} ASSUMED CONSUMER TRUTH**

When you call us for your free in-home consultation, one of our experienced associates will come out to your home and provide the kind of expert advice you're looking for. **VALUE PROPOSITION**

And since all of our associates are specially trained, we guarantee they'll know our product selection inside and out. They'll offer the kind of creative ideas and practical suggestions you're looking for, so you'll have a better idea of what's best for your home at a price that's right for you. **} REASONS TO BELIEVE**

The Right Products

A big part of getting a project done right is having the right products.

ASSUMED CONSUMER TRUTH

When you call us for your free in-home consultation, one of our experienced associates will come out to your home and help you figure out which products are right for you. With our broad selection of materials, styles, and sizes, our skilled professionals will make sure you get the best products at the best price.

VALUE PROPOSITION

REASONS TO BELIEVE

Quality Installation Guaranteed

When it comes to getting a quality installation, you want to know beforehand that everything will be top-notch.

ASSUMED CONSUMER TRUTH

When you call us for a free in-home consultation, you can be confident that the associate who comes out to your home will recommend the right products for your budget and make sure that the contractor you work with will be among the best in your neighborhood. That's because we hand pick our contractors and hold them to a constant customer satisfaction rating, ensuring that they do the perfect job, every time.

REASONS TO BELIEVE

VALUE PROPOSITION

Once the votes are in as to which concept consumers like most, that's when you can develop a brief and share it with Creatives, so that they can then come up with a variety of creative ideas with different kinds of art direction and accompanying lines of copy to make that concept shine.

In short, concept testing helps you identify the single most important thing that consumers want to hear.

It is the strategic "what" that you need to say to get people's attention. Once you know what you need to say, Creatives can figure out "how" you need to say it, developing the final body copy that goes into copy testing.

COPY TESTING

Ads need to be effective. That's why copy testing exists. It's an attempt by Clients to have some kind of assurance that the millions of dollars they're about to spend (or have already spent) on a particular Creative idea is/was worth it.

If Client budgets and timelines permit, copy testing typically takes place at two different stages:

1. During the storyboard stage before the ad gets produced

2. After the ads are on air

The way most Clients see it, copy testing during the storyboard stage is a way for them to make some last minute changes and reduce some of the risk before they spend millions of dollars on production. The way Creatives see it,

it's a process that's going to water down the creative idea. The way Planners see it, it's an opportunity to make sure the primary and secondary messages are coming through.

In general, for broadcast assignments, the Client hires a third party vendor to run copy testing. The third party vendor recruits several hundred respondents among the target market to get in front of their computers and watch a few key storyboard frames (usually in the form of drawings) with a voice over and a little light music in the background. They'll watch the "ad" two, maybe three times in a row, followed by a number of questions.

What you ask in copy testing depends in large part on what your objectives are in the first place. Generally speaking though, most copy testing surveys will typically try to gauge the following:

PERSUASION– measures how much influence the advertising has on respondents' shopping/brand purchase intent later on.

ENJOYMENT – measures how much respondents enjoyed the ad (e.g. found it funny, engaging, exciting, etc.)

ATTENTION VALUE – measures whether the ad held respondents' interest.

BRAND NAME NOTICE – measures whether respondents noticed which brand was delivering the ad.

MEMORABILITY – measures whether or not respondents will actually remember the ad.

PASS-ALONG POTENTIAL – measures whether respondents will share the ad with a friend.

WEAROUT – measures how quickly respondents will tire of an ad and psychologically "tune it out."

You should also know that copy testing results tend to come in large Powerpoint presentations that can range from 40 to 100 slides or more. To make these presentations a little less mind-numbing, there are often a wide variety of colorful charts and graphs. Again, the ultimate goal of copy testing is to make sure the ads are doing what they're supposed to - changing people's attitudes, perceptions and ultimately, their behaviors.

However, as many Planners will tell you, the typical copy testing process is deeply flawed. The biggest problem with copy testing is that it doesn't take place in anything that remotely resembles a real world context. For starters, most people don't watch ads two or three or times in a row when they're watching television at home (or increasingly, on their mobile devices). In the real world, most people either skip through the ads or turn down the volume when an ad comes on. Plus, most people don't really think too much about the primary and secondary messages an ad is trying to tell them. If you ask people to think about what they don't like about an ad, they'll find something to highlight. However, most people don't usually give advertising a second thought.

From an ad agency's perspective, the other major problem with copy testing is that it creates varying degrees of tension between the ad agency, the third party copy testing vendor and the Client. That's because there's the risk that the agency's creative work will be held hostage by the copy testing vendor. For example, if the questions the copy tester asks are poorly worded, consumers may give negative or unfavorable answers about the creative work, which will then make the Clients nervous about going forward with production. Or the answers may make the Client want to start changing all sorts of creative elements, which will probably make the Creatives want to throw themselves out the window.

The point is, entire creative campaigns can either live or die based on a few key frames and a handful of questions during copy testing. That's why it's important for you as a Planner to make friends with the copy testing vendor as well as the research clients who hired the copy testing vendor in the first place. The more you can provide input on everything from screeners to copy testing questions, the more likely your strategic idea and the ensuing creative will actually see the light of day.

THE SCIENCE OF NEW TESTING

A lot of big clients still use copy testing because it's a system that's been around for decades, with norms and results that have been "good enough" for long enough to be considered reliable. But that's beginning to change. In the past several years, a number of new vendors have emerged in the marketplace, bringing innovative techniques and a lot of hard science into the world of copy testing. Instead of asking respondents what they think about a particular ad, respondents are hooked up to neural nodes and their eyes are tracked with gaze tracking technology. Raw neurological (and in some cases physiological) data pours into computers as respondents watch the ads, giving researchers a better read on respondents' emotional reactions to what's being shown. And while the science isn't perfect, it helps researchers read between the lines of all those little white lies and get a better sense of respondents' true reactions.

WHITE PAPERS

Sometimes a Client will notice a trend or hear something in the news and ask either the Account Director or the Account Planner if it's a trend they should be concerned about or if perhaps they should try to leverage it for the benefit of their business. It could be anything from "Should we say things like 'buy local' in our messaging?" to "What are your thoughts on the issue of  corporate social responsibility?" to "What is the Agency's recommendation on the use of QR codes across channels?"

Typically, it's you, the Account Planner, who should pro-actively be bringing important trends to the attention of your Clients, but sometimes they beat you to the punch. If that's the case, even if you don't know anything about it, confirm with them that it is an interesting trend, that you've been keeping an eye on it, and that you'll send them a White Paper ASAP with the Agency's recommendation. This way you can buy yourself the time to do the necessary research, get some key stats and crystallize your thoughts in a concise POV.

Every Planner has a different style or format for writing white papers/POVs, but here's a quick hypothetical example to give you an idea of what they look like.:

POV: Influence of "Buying Local" as Key Drivers of Shopping Behavior

To: Client/Brand name goes here
From: Agency name goes here
Date: Date goes here
Re: Leveraging "Buy Local" Messaging

Background:
Recently, there have been a number of news stories about locally owned businesses and the potential impact of "buy local" messaging. This white paper examines the data surrounding "buy local" messaging and whether it can serve as a key driver of traffic for our brand.

Facts and Figures:
Just one in six adults regularly buys locally available products and services. Although these so-called "true locals" are willing to pay a higher price, most American shoppers don't feel as strongly. *(Source: Always remember to source stats, facts, and figures)*

According to a recent survey, "51% of owners said they believe the 'buy local' sentiment is growing, and 55%

say such campaigns help small businesses compete in challenging economic times." *(Source: Sourcing your data is critical to building trust with the Client)*

In the 2011 Independent Business Survey, cities with active "buy local" campaigns (e.g. Austin, Asheville, Seattle) had businesses that experienced markedly stronger revenue growth compared to businesses located in areas without such a campaign. *(Source: Seriously, if you don't source your stats, your Clients won't believe you)*

What this means for our brand:
The success of "buy local" messaging depends on the category

- Much of the interest in "buying local" has been spurred by the green movement as business owners in food-related categories have attempted to source locally harvested food items. This has created claims of differentiation around improved flavor and reduced carbon-footprints.

- In categories such as apparel, electronics, office supplies, and hardware, the "buy local" sentiment appears to be less of a driver.

The success of "buy local" messaging depends on the city

- The success of "buy local" messaging seems to hinge on whether or not the city as a whole is running a "buy local" campaign. This makes a national "buy local" messaging effort less effective because, in cities where there is no "buy local" campaign or sentiment, "buy local" messaging by individual retailers makes little difference.

Ultimately, for "buy local" messaging to resonate, customers must experience tangible results.

- Whether the results come in the form of improved food flavor (due to local harvesting and freshness) or improved playgrounds at local schools (due to local, charitable giving from local businesses), consumers need tangible proof of how their "buy local" efforts are paying off personally.

POV:

While "buy local" messages may motivate a certain (small) group of consumers and may serve to reinforce the buying habits of existing consumers, such messages are not primary drivers among the vast majority of consumers and would not be an efficient use of mass advertising dollars. As a result, we recommend that any "buy local" messages be used primarily at point of purchase and via social media channels, where media costs are limited and messages can be tailored to specific individuals.

Clients make requests for white papers all the time. The trick is to figure out which ones are genuine opportunities to do something even bigger. A Client once asked whether we thought they were being outflanked by the competition on the sustainability front. The short answer was "Yes. Absolutely." Of course, the Account Director and I could have sent them a one-page white paper explaining the situation and providing a competitive analysis, but we sensed there was a much bigger opportunity to make a meaningful difference to their business, so we bought ourselves some time (about two months) and ended up creating a presentation that went much deeper, offering up fresh insights and new opportunities for the brand that no one in their internal marketing department had fully explored before. So what started out as a simple request became an important internal document that lived on for years, influencing everything from communications to merchandising to R&D and operations.

The best thing you can do as a Planner is to show your Clients that you're always thinking about their business and offering them fresh ideas on a regular basis. As you read reports and follow trends, bookmark the ones you think could be especially beneficial to your Client's business, and think of ways to turn those trends into white papers. You never know where a simple one-page white paper might lead.

BRAINSTORMING

Great Planners understand that to be an indispensable part of the creative process they need to be great at facilitating new ideas (a.k.a. brainstorming). If you build a reputation for helping your Creative team with interesting thought-starters or different ways in, chances are, other Creatives will ask you to join them on a regular basis. However, contrary to popular belief, brainstorms (or ideation sessions as some people call them) involve much more than just throwing people in a room with a couple of easels and dry erase markers and telling them to scribble down whatever thoughts come to mind.

There's an ongoing debate in academic circles about how effective brainstorming actually is, and there are literally hundreds of articles dedicated to different ideation techniques. For now, though, here are a few basics to get you started.

SETTING UP

Make sure the problem and the goals are clearly defined. For example, "Our goal is to come up with a new name for this particular promotion, product or service. Here's the current problem with the name they've got."

Think through your invite list. You don't just want a bunch of copywriters. You want to make sure you've got the right mix of people. People who know about the issue and people who don't. People with different backgrounds. People who think in different ways. Diverse groups and divergent thinking often lead to the most original ideas.

Prepare the room. Find pictures, words, phrases – whatever stimulus you can find that relates to the subject you'll be talking about – and put them up on the walls or scatter them around the table. Do your best to make the room an immersive environment so that as soon as people come in, their minds are marinating in the material you'll be discussing.

Bring an intern and a stopwatch. You'll need someone to take notes and you'll need to make sure you stay on time. It's amazing how fast an hour can go when you're coming up with world changing ideas.

Write down your prompts ahead of time. This is the most time-consuming and critical part of the process, so think through your questions/prompts carefully. Why? Because no matter how creative people are, when it comes to ideating, people inevitably run out of ideas. The tank runs dry. Your job is to keep refueling their imaginations by prompting them to think of the issue from an unexpected or unusual perspective. That's why it's critical for you to think of ways to re-frame the issue ahead of time, so that when you reach those inevitable dead ends, you can phrase the question in a smart and imaginative way and get people to think, "Oh! Well since you put it that way, it makes me think of this…"

THE FIRST FIVE MINUTES

First and foremost, be enthusiastic. Remember that your energy will affect everyone else's energy in the room. If you're enthusiastic, they will be, too. Thank everyone for coming. Introduce people who don't know each other. Give everyone something to write with and write on. Hand out a one-pager with the necessary background information along with the problem and the goals you're trying to achieve. Set the ground rules. No judgment. No censorship. Anything goes. Have fun.

A FEW EFFECTIVE TECHNIQUES

WORD ASSOCIATION

This is a great exercise to get people to loosen up and avoid self-censorship. Start with a word related to the subject that you're brainstorming and go around in a circle, asking each person to say whatever word comes to mind as it relates to the word that was just said.

MIND MAPPING

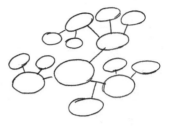

This technique is similar to the word association technique, except that it's a little more structured and a bit more visual. Start with a single word or image in the center of the page. Write down different words on a series of "branches" that relate to that center word. Try using colors to group certain likeminded words/ideas together. As you branch out, you'll start to notice certain ideas or themes emerging as a result.

WRITE & BUILD

Give everyone a 3 x 5 notecard. Have everyone write one idea per note card, writing as many ideas as possible in a span of 3-5 minutes. Collect all the notecards, shuffle them up and pass them around the room, asking each person to build on the idea that's already on the notecard they've just received.

POST-GAME ANALYSIS

When all is said and done at the end of the brainstorm, that doesn't mean you're done. More often than not, some of the best ideas can come after the brainstorm is over, when you're looking at the dozens upon dozens of ideas that were generated during the session. This is the point at which you as a Planner can dig deeper on a particular idea and push it even further. When you feel like you've got something and you've crystallized it into a single compelling sentence or paragraph, share it with the Creatives as a thought-starter. If they like it, they'll run with it. Even if they don't, chances are, it'll spark a conversation, which could result in another big idea.

NEW BUSINESS

If you want to get involved with new business pitches at the agency, you need to let the new business team (and your fellow Planners) know which categories you're most passionate about. That will increase the likelihood that they'll turn to you when it's time to get up to speed on the category, the competition, and consumer behavior within that category.

One thing you should probably know about new business before you get involved, is that it's a fast-moving, all-consuming process that will keep you at the agency at nights and on weekends and lead to very little sleep. That said, if you thrive on intensity and tight timelines, then new business pitches are a great place to sharpen your Planning skills. Not only that, but they'll also give you exposure to a variety of business categories, Account Managers, and Creative teams, which means you'll get to see how different groups think and operate. Plus, C-Suite Executives from the agency are always involved in new business pitches. So if you're part of the new business group, you'll get high profile exposure to agency leadership that you may not normally get.

As a Planner on a new business pitch, you typically have two to three days to get smart about the four Cs and turn around a creative brief. If you're a good presenter who knows more about the category than anybody else, you might even get asked to present key insights and the strategic idea leading up to the creative showcase. If you're young or a relatively inexperienced presenter, then the Planning Director may ask you to sit on the sidelines for the final presentation. Don't take it personally. Just keep raising your hand for new business opportunities and work on becoming a better presenter.

Whether you get to be in the room during the final presentation or not, here is a basic overview of what the new business process looks like from start to finish:

STEP 1: RESPONDING TO THE RFP

RFP stands for Request for Proposal. This is what the Client sends over to see if your agency can actually do what they need. Usually, the new business team will take care of answering the RFP, providing cost structure and case studies from the agency's history that resemble the Clients' situation at hand.

STEP 2: CREDENTIALS/CHEMISTRY CHECK

This is the initial meeting between the prospective Client and the agency. It's a little bit like a first date. That's

ALWAYS THINK BEYOND THE ASSIGNMENT.

why it's called a chemistry check. Both parties want to make sure that they like each other well enough to go on a second date. Typically, the chemistry check lasts about two hours and takes place at the agency. Attendees from the agency side are usually a Creative Director (or two), an Account Director, a Planner, a Media Director and someone from the new business group. During the meeting, the agency and the Client discuss the Client's particular situation and the agency tells the Client a little bit more about the agency's unique perspective on building brands. At GSD&M, it's all about purpose. At Crispin, Porter and Bogusky, it's all about disruption. At BBDO, it's all about "The Work. The Work. The Work."

Even though most agencies have their brand-building philosophy front and center on their websites, the chemistry check is an opportunity to bring that unique philosophy to life via their presentation and their agency "reel" – the work the agency is most proud of. During the meeting, the agency will also try to demonstrate how much it knows about the category and the Client's business, dropping insights and creative tidbits here and there to hint at the strategic and creative opportunities that lay ahead. If all goes well, the Client will be thoroughly impressed and ask the agency on a second date.

STEP 2.5: BRIEFING AND BRAINSTORMING

Right after the chemistry check, that's when Planning goes into high gear, doing primary research and working with the media team to develop a rough target segmentation so that everyone has a decent idea of who the target audience is. Again, how much time you have to do all this depends on the new business timeline. The tissue session could be anywhere from one week to one month away. If you have just one week, you basically have 24-48 hours to turn the brief around. If you have one month, you have more time. During new business, normal working hours cease to exist. It's constant collaboration with lots of check-ins, lots of late nights and lots of catered food.

STEP 3: THE TISSUE SESSION

The term "tissue session" comes from the 1950s when unfinished creative concepts were hand drawn on tissue paper. The tissue session during a new business pitch is more or less the same thing. Creative ideas are still relatively loose, but they'll give the Client a sense of what the campaign direction will look like – a manifesto, a couple of TV spots, a couple of digital components, etc. The tissue session could happen at the Agency or at the Client's headquarters. If it happens at the Clients' headquarters, there's usually some logistical planning that needs to take place. What does the presentation room look like? How big is it? What's the lighting like? Who's going to sit where? What does the new business team need to bring (e.g. projector, television, boards, etc.) to make it an amazing presentation?

During the tissue session, the Planner takes the Client through the brief and then passes the baton to the Creatives, at which point the Creative team presents the work and the agency gets feedback. It's important during the tissue session to leave a lot of time for the Clients to talk, so that they can give everyone a much better idea of what they're sensitive to — things like language, tone, certain likes/dislikes, etc.

STEP 3.5: REVISING FOR THE FINAL PITCH

Once you get the Client's feedback, it's time to make some decisions. You can go back and scrap whole campaigns, or you can just tweak and fix little things here and there. Sometimes, you create new campaigns. Or sometimes you flesh out a campaign idea that you held back and never showed during the tissue session. As a Planner, there's an opportunity for you between the tissue session and the final pitch to do some quick tests on manifestos and ideas. It's not the most in-depth research, but you can usually get some animatics/video boards in front of consumers to get their reactions. This can help Creatives make last minute revisions before the final presentation.

STEP 4: THE FINAL PRESENTATION

The final pitch is usually a two hour presentation where the creative idea must be completely blown out, including tv, print, out of home, digital, interactive, apps, microsites, guerilla events, etc. Typically, you've got 20-30 minutes for setup, an hour for creative, and thirty minutes for discussion.

A big part of winning new business is how well you sell the presentation. A winning pitch is 40% strategy, 40% creative idea and 20% theatre. For final pitches, most big agencies go all out. I once heard that for an insurance company pitch, the agency that won contracted a local band to write a new, original jingle for the brand. When the Clients came out of the presentation room, the entire agency was standing around in the lobby. At first, a solo guitarist stepped out of the crowd and began to sing the jingle. When he reached the chorus line, the entire agency along with a professional church choir joined in with him. The moral of the story: it's important to remember that Clients are people too, and can be moved by a powerful performance.

STEP 5: THE DECISION

If you win, more often than not the Clients will tell you right away, sometimes as soon as you're done presenting. If you lose, sometimes the Client won't say anything. Sometimes, you'll have to find out by reading about it in AdAge. If you win, then it's time for the agency and the Client to start negotiations – talking about things like scope of work, staffing plans, etc.

***

One thing to always remember about new business pitches—there is no magic formula. That's because there's a wide variety of reasons why Clients put their businesses up for review. Sometimes, there's a new CEO or CMO who just wants to change things up. Other times, Clients want to light a fire under their existing agency and maybe even see if they can drive the cost down. And then there are those times when Clients are looking for groundbreaking new work. That means this is the one time they're not playing it safe, so do everything you can to help your team go big.

Also, as more and more brands go global, you'll need to keep in mind that the campaign will likely extend beyond the borders of North America. So do your best to develop strategies that are rooted in a universal human truth. Put your global lens on and be prepared to test the campaign idea in other countries, languages and cultures.

At the end of the day, new business is the lifeblood of any agency. Most big agencies have anywhere from 5-10 new business prospects each quarter. If you can get involved in at least one of those new business pitches each quarter, even if it's just in a supporting role, you'll be a much better Planner as a result.

Courtesy of The Awesome World of Advertising

POSITIONING

At its most basic, positioning is all about claiming prime real estate in people's minds. It's about owning a concept, an idea, an emotion. To get a better understanding of how positioning works, look no further than the world of bottled water. From a functional standpoint, each bottle of water does the same thing. It keeps you hydrated. But from an emotional or psychological standpoint, the positioning opportunities for bottled water are as varied as the people who drink it. That's where Planning comes in.

Each of the above brands owns a particular territory in people's minds. And this small group is just the tip of the iceberg. This doesn't even begin to include sparkling water or the new crop of "enhanced" waters like Smart Water, Vitamin Water, Oxygenated water, etc.

One way to see potential positioning opportunities is to plot the competition on an X-Y axis:

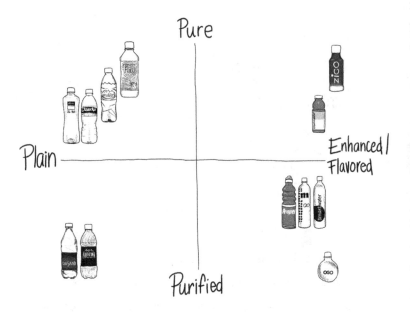

The important thing to remember is that the "white space" or positioning opportunity will change based on the values on your axes. For example, if you change the X axis to reflect a spectrum of charity vs. non-charity water (as you see on the following page), then Ethos Water stands alone.

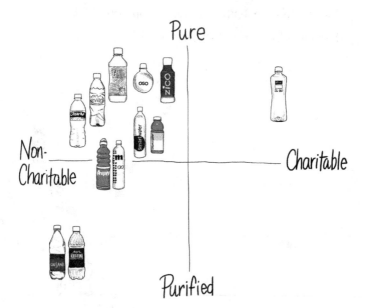

Pure · Non-Charitable · Charitable · Purified

When you do a positioning exercise like this, the values you place on each axis become extremely important. To figure out which values to use, you're probably going to have to do some qualitative and quantitative research. Because while Ethos may have virtually no competition within the "charity" spectrum, research may reveal that the vast majority of people are more interested in enhanced water over charitable contributions, which would make enhanced water a more strategic, long term positioning.

Beer is another great example when it comes to positioning. Sure there are differences in the way beer tastes, but what often differentiates each beer brand is not so much the taste, but how the brand is perceived in the eyes of consumers. Again, that's where Planning comes in. Ultimately, the major points of differentiation are rooted in the psychological identity or emotional aspirations of the brand's target audience.

All of the above are good examples of brand positioning, but I find Dos Equis especially interesting in terms of how it differentiates itself creatively. It's sophisticated without being stuffy. It's approachable, but it's not exactly laid back. It's meant to be for every man, but it's spokesman is an older man who's well-traveled, wise, and always the life of the party. With smart positioning and clever creative, he is "the most interesting man in the world." And the complexity of his sophistication is summed up by the line he says at the end of each commercial, "I don't always drink beer, but when I do, I prefer Dos Equis."

UNDERSTANDING POSITIONING IS EASY.

CARVING OUT A SUCCESSFUL POSITIONING IS HARD.

Another way to approach positioning is by creating what's called a positioning triangle. Different Planners will put different questions at each of the three points, but here's an example of what a positioning triangle might look like.

Is it Believable?
Does it fit with our brand?

Does it Resonate with Our Target?
Does it line up with a consumer insight?

Is it Uniquely Ownable?
Does it differentiate us from our competition?

If, after you write your positioning statement, you can give an unequivocal yes to all three questions, then you're probably onto something.

So how do you write a brand positioning in the first place? Every Planner has a slightly different method or format, but at its most basic, a classic brand positioning looks something like this:

For (target audience who _____), (your brand) is the only one that delivers (benefit/point of difference) because only (your brand) is (reason to believe).

So let's say you're writing a positioning statement for a medium-sized bank. It might say:

For small business owners who take pride in their business, our bank is the only bank that can give them the dedicated attention and service that they deserve, because our bank is the only one that understands that when your business is your livelihood, it's not just business. It's personal.

A shorthand version of this might be:

For small business owners, we understand business isn't just business. It's personal.

For many Clients, it often helps if you have a paragraph (some call it a manifesto) that accompanies the positioning statement, to bring it to life just a little bit more, highlighting some of the additional reasons to believe.

So for the above example, an accompanying paragraph might look something like this:

You want to work with someone who knows your name and your business, not just your account number; someone who will treat you with courtesy and respect no matter how big your bank account is, someone who will answer the phone and answer your questions instead of making you navigate your way through an automated phone tree. At our bank, we know that running your business isn't just a job. It's a passion. It's your livelihood. Which is why, at our bank, we don't just do business. We make your business our business. We make it personal.

***

It's important to keep in mind that a brand's positioning can change with the times. After all, consumers, competitors, the category and the culture are always changing, too, shifting like giant sand dunes.

At the end of the day, the brand you're working on must stay ahead of the prevailing cultural winds, or else be buried and forgotten. That's what great positioning can do. It keeps your brand relevant, top of mind, and on the tips of people's tongues.

BRAND ARCHITECTURE

Great brands are like great buildings. Every room and design element has a reason. Long before the foundation gets poured or the first beam goes up, great architects develop blueprints, providing guidance on key features, with a particular purpose, philosophy or ethos at their core.

Unfortunately, only a select number of brands seem to understand and embrace this metaphor. That's because most brands didn't start off thinking of themselves as brands. They started off as a simple business that then grew at an exponential rate, and somewhere along the way, someone suggested that it might be helpful if they had some kind of unifying brand philosophy or architecture to guide them.

As Planners, we're the ones who typically get asked to develop the blueprints after the building has already been

 built. In other words, we're asked to explain why all the different pieces exist, which means that nine times out of ten, you end up with a brand architecture that seems to defy logic or reason.

There's no doubt that this is one of the most challenging parts of being a Planner. To make sense out of an architecture that doesn't appear to make sense. But that's one of the many things we're asked to do — take a step back from the daily chaos and provide some kind of underlying structure that everyone can turn to and rely upon.

Brand architectures come in all shapes and forms, from pyramids to interlocking gears to spoke and wheel structures. Use whatever visual metaphor tickles your fancy. Just remember that Clients will come to you every now and again with exciting news, saying they've decided to pursue a new brand partnership or that they've signed a contract with a celebrity spokesperson and they want to see how it's going to fit into the current brand architecture. So whichever organizing principles and visuals you decide to use, just make sure they're flexible enough to add new elements every few months.

SEGMENTATION STUDIES

Many Clients will tell you during a project kickoff call that the target is "everyone." That might be because they haven't done a segmentation study. Or maybe they did one a long time ago, but the segments they ended up with weren't very well-defined and were therefore not very meaningful. As a Planner, you should see this as a huge opportunity. Not because you'll necessarily be doing the segmentation yourself, but because you can influence what goes into the next segmentation study so that you can end up getting more meaningful results.

Whether the bulk of the segmentation study is done by you or a third party vendor depends on the Client, the agency and the budget. Sometimes, the Planning department controls the entire segmentation from start to finish. Other times, the Client does most of the legwork and the Planning department plays a supportive role, nudging things this way or that. If the segmentation study is done well, it will help you identify your most valuable current and potential customers. It will also give you a set of very specific target descriptions that will not only be invaluable on future creative briefs, but will also help your Clients develop innovative product or service offerings.

A thorough segmentation study usually takes several months to complete and can cost hundreds of thousands of dollars. That's because it's a combination of qualitative and quantitative research, as well as Client orientation workshops. For many businesses, the segmentation study becomes the strategic foundation for their organization's future growth. That said, because segmentation studies are such massive undertakings with such big price tags, a lot of Clients don't do them or do them very rarely.

Every segmentation study looks a little different, but to get a better sense of the different stages, from start to finish, here's a bird's eye view.

PROJECT KICKOFF	VALUES RESEARCH	ONLINE SURVEY	DATA WORKSHOP	IMPLEMENTATION WORKSHOP
Identify & clarify objectives	Establish screening criteria & recruitment	Create and field online survey, with learnings from values research	Work with client to plan and execute workshop	Interactive workshops with key stakeholders to aid clients in their adoption and value-added use of segments across departments
Review existing information	Develop discussion guide	Create report/ analytic plan	Conduct one-day workshop with key stakeholders	
Identify ingoing hypotheses	Create values maps	Develop multiple segmentation solutions	Determine best segmentation solution	
Determine segmentation strategy		Develop reporting tool that will define and chart segments for each solution	Identify other key issues to address in final report	
Discuss screening criteria for qualitative & quantitative phases				

By the end of the study, after all the research is done, you should have several distinct segments. Here's an example of five key segments for a hypothetical grocery brand.

PRACTICAL PAM

Suburban mom with two kids

Always shops with a grocery list

Doesn't typically purchase household or personal care items

Opportunity: increase basket size beyond traditional grocery categories

BUSY BONNIE

Fresh out of college/grad school

Cooks 2-3 times per week

Heavy mobile user

Looks for fresh, on-the-go meals

Opportunity: highlight ready-made meals and increase usage of grocery store app

TRENDY TRICIA

Established professional

Likes to entertain guests at home

Active user of Pinterest for recipes

Early adopter of the latest food trends

Opportunity: increase shopping frequency by focusing on party platters, decorations, and catering

HEALTHY HEATHER

Stay-at-home mom

Shops 3+ times per week

Buys seasonal/organic produce

Often shops at Farmer's Markets

Opportunity: introduce her to private label line of organic products to increase overall basket size

ANALOG ALICE

Retired/Empty nester

Middle income

Coupon clipper

Looks for the best deals in
weekend circulars

Frequently pays with cash

Shops all parts of the store

Opportunity: encourage her to enroll in rewards program
to provide more relevant deals via direct mail campaigns

As you may have noticed, these particular segments are
pretty heavy on alliteration. That's relatively common with
segmentation studies, probably because it makes each
segment easier to remember. That said, once you have
a handful of segments, that doesn't mean your job as a
Planner is actually done. To make these segments something
Creatives can actually use, you're going to have to go one step
further and bring these segments to life.

DEVELOPING PERSONAS

Between the ethnographies, the focus groups, the segmentation study, the digital data, and all your secondary sources, you've probably got more information on your target customers than J. Edgar Hoover had in all his manila folders at the FBI. So now what do you do with all that information? If the assignment is a national ad campaign requiring a big, breakthrough idea, most Creatives will just want to know the cultural, category, or consumer insight. However, if the assignment involves multiple digital touchpoints, then chances are, you'll need to create personas. Similar to creative briefs, every agency has a different layout when it comes to customer personas. However, here's the basic information you'll need:

Persona #1
Profile pic

⋮ NAME ⋮
Age
Education Level
JOB TITLE
Household Income
Family Info

Topline Goals
Topline Motivations
Major obstacles / fears / concerns
when it comes to making decisions

Quote that sums up this person's experience / unmet need.

DEVICES USED
(eg smartphone, laptop, tablet, etc.)

Most Visited Websites

Social Media Behavior
Sites used most often
#Hours per day / week
Typical Activities

Customer Scenario:

A short description of a typical "day in the life of" this particular persona, highlighting:
- a situation where she would come into contact with the category / brand
- her biggest motivations / concerns when making a decision

The most important thing to remember is that personas are living, breathing documents and should be updated frequently. In addition to broad cultural shifts, competition within the category can impact customers' attitudes and behaviors, which will have an impact on your personas. To keep your personas current, you must maintain a consistent dialogue with customers, which is where social media monitoring tools and rolling online focus groups can help in a big way.

The biggest challenge for Planners when it comes to developing personas is figuring out which information is going to be most useful to the Creatives and the media team. That's why you have to be great at separating the wheat from the chaff, boiling things down to their essence, and seeing the difference between insightful, meaningful nuggets and fool's gold.

The bottom line: before you run off and spend hours developing these kinds of documents, check with your Creatives and understand what it is they actually need.

SEGMENTATION VS. PERSONAS: WHAT'S THE DIFFERENCE?

Market segmentations are necessary to identify how big your target market is.

For example, a traditional market segmentation study might reveal that 53% of drivers aged 25–54 say that they sometimes get distracted while driving, and that side air bags would affect their purchase decision.

A persona, on the other hand, might show that Jim, aged 37, uses his iPod and cell phone every time he drives by himself, and he's concerned that this makes him a more unsafe driver. He wishes that there were something he could buy that could meet his communication and listening needs, while also helping him deal with potentially unsafe situations.

With personas, you get richer motivational information that traditional market segmentation can't usually provide. This can help with innovative product/service development and website design. It can also provide richer, more relevant scenarios when it comes to messaging.

Typically, though, segmentation studies and personas go hand in hand. They're like chips and salsa. They go better together.

CONSUMER DECISION PROCESS MAPS

In every category – from auto to apparel to electronics to financial services - the path to purchase is always a little different. That's because each category has a different set of target consumers and different purchase occasions. For example, on the following page is a hypothetical consumer decision map for the home improvement category.

If we were making a map for a popular soda brand, the map would look completely different. The phases would be different. The media channels would be different. The customers' unmet needs would be different. But maps like these are where all those focus groups, ethnographies, segmentations, and website data come into play. By carefully studying people's decision-making processes, both in terms of how they think and how they behave, Account Planners, Media Planners, and UX Planners are able to create more accurate decision making maps, which can then influence creative messaging and media placement.

Ultimately, when you have a map that shows where consumers are in their decision making process, you have a better chance of getting them onto the path you want them to take.

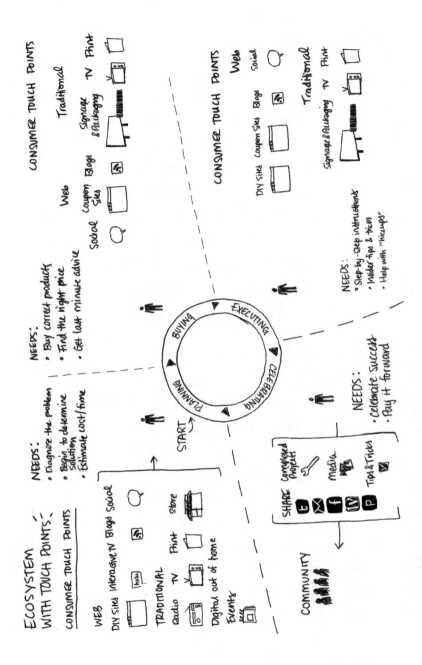

ECOSYSTEM
WITH TOUCH POINTS

CONSUMER TOUCH POINTS

WEB
DIY Sites Interactive TV Blogs Social

TRADITIONAL
Radio TV Print Store

Digital out of home

Events

START
PLANNING

NEEDS:
• Diagnose the problem
• Begin to determine solution
• Estimate cost/time

CONSUMER TOUCH POINTS

Social   Web
Coupon Sites   Blogs

Traditional
Signage & Packaging   TV   Print

BUYING

NEEDS:
• Buy correct product
• Find the right price
• Get last minute advice

EXECUTING

CELEBRATING

CONSUMER TOUCH POINTS

Web
DIY Sites Coupon Sites Blogs   Social

Traditional
Signage & Packaging   TV   Print

NEEDS:
• Step-by-step instructions
• Insider tips & tricks
• Help with "hiccups"

SHARE
Completed Project
Media
Tips & Tricks

NEEDS:
• Celebrate Success
• Pay it forward

COMMUNITY

PRO BONO WORK

Just about every agency takes on pro bono clients from time to time. That's usually because someone in the C-suite serves on the board of a nonprofit (or two) and wants to help them out. So whenever you hear about a pro bono opportunity in the building, raise your hand and get involved. Why? Because more often than not, pro bono work is a win-win for everyone involved. The nonprofit gets access to top talent, Creatives and Planners get a chance to do something that nourishes the soul, and the agency usually gets buzz-worthy work that they can enter into award shows.

More specifically, for you, as a Planner, it'll be an opportunity to work closely with additional Creative teams as well as some of the C-suite executives inside the agency. It's a chance to get noticed for your inspiring insights and your amazing collaborative skills, which could pay dividends in the future, when another project comes up and the CEO (Chief Executive Officer) or CCO (Chief Creative Officer) recommends you for the job. It's also an opportunity to work in an environment with fewer layers, meaning you're more likely to be working directly with the leaders of the nonprofit rather than junior Clients. That means there's less of a chance that the work will get killed or watered down because there's less bureaucracy to deal with. It also means a little more pressure for you as a Planner, but if you ask me, that's a good thing. It's good practice. It'll force you to sharpen your presentation skills and get you to explain things as clearly and concisely as possible since you'll be dealing with high-level executives who are always pressed for time.

So if you have the time and the drive, and if you're interested in using your talents for the greater good, let everyone who you work with (especially your fellow Planners) know about your nonprofit passions. That way, the next time a pro bono account comes through the door, you'll be much more likely to get tapped for the job, either as an assistant or as the lead Strategic Planner. And who knows? If the work is great and your agency ends up submitting it to a show, you just might end up with a prestigious industry award, which can work wonders for your career.

AWARD SHOWS

Agencies love to win awards. That's because awards get industry attention and have a tendency to bring in new business. If you're on an account that has developed some extremely creative, highly effective work, chances are you'll be asked to do the write-up for the award show entry. If your agency has a dedicated awards department, find out who runs it and make friends with them. Chances are, they'll have back issues of award show annuals, DVD reels, and subscriptions to inspirational publications like Communication Arts, Luerzers Archive, Creativity, and more. Looking at other award-winning entries will give you an idea of how to structure your own. If your agency doesn't have a dedicated awards department, do your best to start one, even if it's housed in your personal cubicle. Talk to the Planning Department Director and see if there's money in the budget for subscriptions to some of those inspirational magazines. Even if you don't have an award winning campaign, you can still get some amazing ideas from those publications, which can impact your own thinking as a Planner. Whenever you see, hear or experience impressive work, see if you can reverse engineer the idea all the way back to its original mind-blowing insight.

Here's a short list of some of the most competitive award shows in the industry. If you're ever feeling down or disheartened about a Client who "just doesn't get it", turn to these pages for rejuvenation and inspiration.

Effies	Clios	Adweek's Media
Jay Chiat Awards for	One Show	Plan of the Year
Strategic Excellence	Cannes	IAB MIXX
	Art Director's Club	OMMA
	Communication Arts	
	Design & Art Direction	
	ADDY Awards	
	Andys	

IF YOU WANT TO BE THE BEST, YOU HAVE TO SURROUND YOURSELF WITH THE BEST WORK THAT'S OUT THERE.

PART IV: TRICKS OF THE TRADE

ASKING DIFFERENT QUESTIONS

Most Planners will agree that the best insights are the result of asking questions that are fundamentally different from the ones everyone else is asking. Here are a few questions that will help you frame the brand's business challenge in a new way.

"What business are we *really* in?"

Clients may think you're joking when you ask this question, so you have to be careful when and how you ask it. However, the purpose of the question is to uncover the brand's reason for being. After all, Nike isn't just in the apparel business. And Apple isn't just in the electronics business. Both brands are selling something much bigger than a commodity. They're selling an idea. They're selling a world view. If you can reframe your Client's business by asking this question, you'll be one step closer to what might be an industry-changing insight.

"What's the business problem we're trying to solve?"

A lot of times, Clients will tell you they need a campaign. And more often than not, agencies are happy to oblige. That is, after all, how agencies make their money. However, sometimes, an advertising campaign is not what the Client needs at all. Sometimes, what they need is a re-evaluation of the business problem, along with a solution that goes much deeper than an advertising campaign. For example, Tesla Motors could have spent millions on an advertising campaign to raise awareness about their electric cars. But raising awareness wouldn't have solved the real business problem that Tesla faced, which is that consumers are unfamiliar with and skittish about electric car technology. To solve that problem, Tesla needed to do more than make a bunch of television spots and print ads. They needed to create engaging experiences where people could get their questions about electric cars answered. That's why they've created immersive store experiences in malls across America. It's still a marketing solution, but it's a solution that gets at the heart of Tesla's unique business problem.

"Are we giving people stories/experiences that are worth retelling?"

Which is the more memorable experience? Watching a television ad about an electric car? Or getting in the driver's seat of an electric car and taking it for a twenty minute test drive at 70 mph? Which one are you more likely to tell your friends about? Sometimes, a clever commercial – like the Old Spice Guy commercial – can get people talking. But more and more these days, with the market completely cluttered with forgettable advertising, it's authentic, memorable experiences that matter most. As the old Chinese proverb goes, "Tell me and I'll forget. Show me and I may remember. Involve me and I'll understand."

"What would the world look like if we took _____ away?"

Also known as a deprivation study, and usually part of an ethnography, this deceptively simple question has a way of getting people to open up about their true feelings for a brand or product. In some cases, entire campaigns have been built on the backs of deprivation studies, from the "Got Milk" campaign to Burger King's "Whopper Freakout." Obviously, people will always be upset if you take away one of their favorite brands, but the trick with this question is to figure out what exactly they feel is missing or what makes that brand or product so special.

"How can we challenge the pre-existing cultural or category convention?"

Whether it's UKotex or Shredded Mini Squares or IKEA's award winning lamp spot, these brands all have one thing in common. With a bit of humor and some serious brass, they poked fun at people's pre-conceived notions of what's "normal".

PLANNING RESOURCES

As mentioned before, Planners are voracious consumers of the printed word. Here are just a few resources most Planners use to find important stats and get up to speed on the latest trends.

NEWS SOURCES
New York Times
Wall Street Journal
Washington Post
The Daily Beast
Huffington Post
Reuters
BBC News

MAGAZINES
Wired
Fast Company
Good Magazine
Newsweek
Time
The Week
Harvard Business
Review

TREND BLOGS
PSFK.com
Buzzfeed.com
Digg.com
Reddit.com
Crowwsnest.com
Viralblog.com
TrendsSpotting.com

DATABASES
Pew Research Center
Harris Interactive
Gallup
Nielsen
Marketing Daily
Deloitte
Experian
Accenture

SUBSCRIPTIONS
Mintel
Warc
Contagious
Iconoculture
Yankelovich
Forrester
eMarketer
GFK Roper
Kantar Retail
McKinsey Quarterly
AAAA

Depending on the category you're working on, there will be other specialized sources that you'll want to use. Plus, new resources are coming out all the time, so make sure you refresh your list at least once a month. Ask your fellow Planners and Creatives what magazines and blogs they read to stay inspired. It's always a good conversation starter and it'll give you a better sense for what it is they're most interested in.

PRESENTING LIKE A PLANNER

What really separates a good Planner from a great Planner is storytelling. Good Planners know how to do research, find insights and synthesize information. Great Planners, however, know how to take all that information and tell a compelling story. At the end of the day, great storytelling is rooted in simplicity. If you're a great storyteller, you don't need software. You should be able to tell an effective story on the back of a napkin.

Here are a few tips to keep in mind as you attempt to tell your own unique stories.

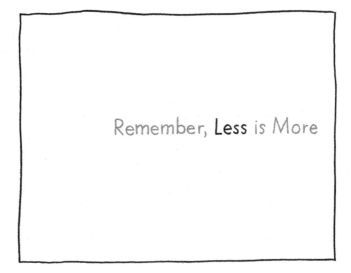

Remember, **Less** is More

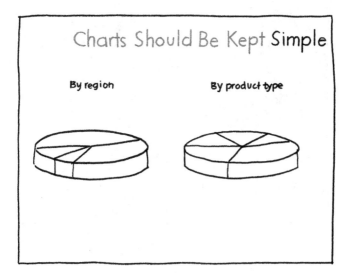

Charts Should Be Kept **Simple**

By region   By product type

Sometimes, pictures can say it all

(See next slide)

"A great quote all by itself is worth a thousand charts.

— Insert name here

Always Tell a Great Story

A presentation should flow seamlessly;
no jumping from thought to thought

Use your headlines to say something important,
not just announce a topic such as "NewTrends"

If you can put a POV in your headlines
your presentations will be far more interesting

ADVICE FOR PLANNERS FROM PLANNERS

Be patient. At first it's hard to see the big picture and it may seem like you're not adding value or playing a significant role, but planning takes time. Everyone in the field talks about how they had no idea what planning really was the first year. Not only is our discipline a difficult one to grasp, but everyone's approach varies and takes a while to hone. Just be patient, listen, and be willing to get your hands dirty. The more you get to help, the quicker you'll hit your stride.

— Jasmin Esquivel, Senior Brand Strategist,
Publicis New York

Find a more experienced planner that you trust to be brutally honest in critiquing your work -- it's the best way to learn. Stay close to creatives...it's amazing how a little creativity can transform a brief. Use the sometimes unstructured nature of planning to bring your passions into your job.

— Jenna Goldstein Rounds, Planning Director,
Young & Rubicam New York

The greatest day to be a planner is when you're responsible for something that directly leads to a brilliant breakthrough idea. Something wholly original, something so inspiring to your agency team that the idea leaps from something conceptual to something real while still in your mind and the content it will yield almost creates itself in front of your eyes. Your thinking, your analysis, your hard work is the the seed; the beginning of something big that you will be proud of and build your career around. They are special moments so enjoy them.

There will be other days though, if you're fortunate to be surrounded by other original thinkers, that you're not directly responsible for an idea that will make your client famous; but you still have a critical job to do to make a budding idea real. You can explore the idea, refine the idea, strengthen the idea and sell the hell out of the idea to a skeptical, cautious or discriminating client by proving or demonstrating the merits of the idea. You're role is to water an idea and help it blossom into memorable and meaningful work.

Frequently remind yourself: sometimes the seed, sometimes the water.

— John D'Acierno, SVP/Group Planning Director

Throughout your career, you will be expected to contribute to many consumer research projects. It's important that you don't merely treat these assignments as fact-finding missions. If that were all that was expected of you, then your job title would be Market Researcher, not Account Planner. Yes, you find the facts and uncover the truth, but ultimately, the value you really add is the perspective you bring to the research – both in its design and in its outcome.

Yes, it takes intelligence to do what we do, but there's no shortage of intelligence in our industry. You will prove your worth by having a fresh perspective – one that shines a light on some things while cropping out others – to position all of those facts and truths into something new, unique, powerful, game-changing, and truly great. Your responsibility as a planner is to shine a whole new light on the truth. Make that your true north, and you'll be well on your way to developing a Planner's perspective.

— Eddy Hodgson, Brand Planning Director,
The Richards Group

ADVICE FOR PLANNERS FROM CREATIVES

Don't be afraid to be speak up. And ask to be part of the review process. Just because you don't have the word 'creative' in your title doesn't mean you can't be thoughtful about a creative idea. After all, as much as creatives want to make cool stuff, we want to make cool stuff that delivers results even more.

— Heidi Waldusky, Executive Creative Director,
Havas Worldwide New York

The more succinct the brief, the better. We'd rather ask you questions than sort through a fifty page deck. The better the insight, the better our work will be.

— Evan Brown, Associate Creative Director,
Saatchi & Saatchi Los Angeles

It's been said that the very best Art Directors are great Copywriters and the very best Copywriters are great Art Directors. I believe the same theory holds true between Planners and Creatives.

— Ben Thoma, Senior Art Director

You'll know you've written a great brief when the creatives start coming up with ideas before the briefing is over. You'll know your brief sucks if all you get are questions. Or worse, silence.

— Jenn Shreve, Associate Creative Director,
Razorfish New York

You need to be curious. If you've never asked how does that work, what's in there, or what's under those clothes, then how can you find the truth in an idea?

— David Weinstock, Executive Creative Director,
MRY New York

Don't confuse the way you brief the creative team with the way you brief the client, and vice versa.

— Christopher Cole, SVP/Creative Director,
Leo Burnett Chicago

Boil your brief down to one sentence. Throw out the marketing speak and write it like a real person would say it. That line is the springboard to great work.

— Brian Thompson, Associate Creative Director, T3 Austin

SUGGESTED READING

Magazines, newspapers, and blogs are a Planner's best friends when it comes to staying current on the latest trends. However, here's a list of great reads that will help you think differently and make you into an even better Planner. This list is by no means exhaustive, but it's a good head start. To add to this list with recommendations of your own, visit www.practicalplanningbook.com/resources.

Zag: The Number One Strategy of High-Performance Brands
Marty Neumeier

Positioning: The Battle for Your Mind
Al Ries, Jack Trout, and Phillip Kotler

The Intention Economy: When Customers Take Charge
Doc Searls

Why We Buy: The Science Of Shopping
Paco Underhill

Predictably Irrational: The Hidden Forces That Shape Our Decisions
Dan Ariely

Purple Cow: Transform Your Business by Being Remarkable
Seth Godin

Marketing Metaphoria: What Deep Metaphors Reveal About the Minds of Consumers
Gerald Zaltman and Lindsay H. Zaltman

The Ten Faces of Innovation: IDEO's Strategies for Defeating the Devil's Advocate and Driving Creativity Throughout Your Organization
Tom Kelley

The Culting of Brands: Turn Your Customers into True Believers
Doug Atkins

Brand Portfolio Strategy: Creating Relevance, Differentiation, Energy, Leverage, and Clarity
David A. Aaker

How Customers Think: Essential Insights into the Mind of the Market
Gerald Zaltman

Truth, Lies and Advertising : The Art of Account Planning
Jon Steel

INDEX

NOTES

CHRIS KOCEK is the founder & CEO of Gallant, a strategy and design studio dedicated to building brands for a better world. Prior to starting Gallant, Chris worked as a strategic Planner at advertising agencies in NYC and Austin, developing nationally recognized campaigns for a number of Fortune 500 brands and highly respected nonprofits, including AARP, Lowe's Home Improvement, Hyatt Hotels, Ace Hardware, John Deere, and The Christopher and Dana Reeve Foundation. In addition to guest lecturing at the University of Texas at Austin, Chris is a public speaker whose talks on creativity and innovation have been featured at strategic symposiums around the country as well as TEDx.

For more practical Planning tips and resources, visit:
www.practicalplanningbook.com

CPSIA information can be obtained
at www.ICGtesting.com
Printed in the USA
LVHW081746150721
692810LV00003B/41